"2014" Daily Reflections of Inspirations

Book Your Face Here!

Demonn McNeill

authorHOUSE®

AuthorHouse™ LLC
1663 Liberty Drive
Bloomington, IN 47403
www.authorhouse.com
Phone: 1-800-839-8640

Published by AuthorHouse 12/10/2013

ISBN: 978-1-4918-4267-6 (sc)
ISBN: 978-1-4918-4266-9 (e)

Library of Congress Control Number: 2013922691

About The Author

Demonn McNeill was born February 26, 1972 to the Late Jennie Pearl McNeill. I am residence of St. Pauls, North Carolina. I am currently the Pastor of Total Praise & Deliverance Church of God Founded By Jesus Christ Located in Raeford, North Carolina. I am currently the Assistant General Superintendent of the Church of God Founded By Jesus Christ, Inc.

In December of 1996, I accepted my call into the ministry. So on March 9, 1997, I preached my first message entitled "Where Do We Go From Here." It really blessed a lot of people. God has anointed, appointed and chosen me to spread the Gospel of Jesus Christ. It has not been easy but I went through in order to get through so I can count it all Joy even in the present time. I love encouraging people and let them know that there is a bright side to every situation and circumstance in their life. So the thoughts in my head will reach this book to inspire, motivate, and encourage each of you on a daily basis.

Dedication

This book is dedicated to all my readers who took time everyday to read my motivational and inspirational thoughts that God gave me daily. Before I turned on my computer I would pray and say, “Lord, what do I need to post today to touch or impact someone’s life?” He gave me just what to say to each of you. So I decided to compile this my 3rd book to allow you to hold on to the memories and make it through each day. Some days I have added scriptures so that you can read a portion of God’s Word every day. Most passages I have drawn from the book of Psalm. I encourage each of you to hold on to what you have. So I dedicated this book not only to each individual but I dedicate this Book Back To God whom has given me the original sayings to spread His Word through Facebook.

This book is written in memory of
The World Greatest Mother, who encouraged and
inspired many people through her life:

The Late Jennie Pearl McNeill

October 14, 1943 thru October 14, 2001

Preface

The purpose of this book is to encourage believers on a daily basis to be motivated and inspired knowing that God is going to bring each of us through. Facebook isn't a bad thing it's what the people do on facebook make it bad. I choose to use it as a ministry and touch the hearts of people through what God tells me to say. There is a section under each day that you can reflect on what great and wonderful things God has blessed you with and be able to record His goodness. When I wake up in the morning, I say, "Lord what would you have me to say to us this morning to get us through the day. I do not mind posting regardless of the time. There are some people who go to work earlier than others; therefore, I feel within my heart they need the message before going to their place of employment. So Book Your Face in this book and allow God to speak to your heart, soul, and spirit as you think and reflect on His goodness. If I can touch or help one person along life's journey then I know that my living will not be in vain.

Acknowledgements

I would like to acknowledge everyone that took the time every day to read my inspirational messages from God. It is because of you, that I was able to write this book. My three early main supporters go to: Deon Jones, Tinishia McMillian, and Alishia Tolson. There are many others of you that read them but some of you all may not want to hit the like button but at least you get the message. I always have the support of my family, the church I love and hold very dear to my heart, Total Praise & Deliverance Church of God Founded by Jesus Christ, Inc., (BABM) Build A Bear Ministry, HUSTY (Helping Us Save The Youth). My 3 Godparents Mr. & Mrs. James Johnson, Mr. & Mrs. Louis Thomas and Mr. & Mrs. Thomas Clawson. I love you all so much.

December 31

Enjoying the day! Getting ready to close out this year in 5 hours and 55 minutes . . . . Watch God do a great and awesome thing in the lives of His people for the 2013 year . . . Whatever God is doing in this season, please don't do it without me . . . . I AM GLAD I AM INCLUDED IN HIS PLAN . . . . From January 1, 2013 up to this present time God Has Truly Been Good To Me. I thank God for the plans He has for me for the year that lies ahead for us. I am Moving Forward With A Diving Purpose. As Dorothy Norwood states, "I am not going to let nothing happen to me this YEAR that me and the good Lord can't handle. Happy New Year! We will be singing, dancing and praising God at Total Praise and Deliverance as the New Year comes in.

Time of Reflections

____

____

____

____

____

Let's Begin As We Close Out One Year
And
Enter Into A New Year!
Let's Leave The Past in The Past and
MOVE FORWARD WITH A DIVINE PURPOSE!

Month One

January

January 1

Happy New Year Tonight, Today & FOREVER . . . . GOD BLESS YOU ALL AND KEEP YOU SAFE IN HIS CARE . . . . Just expect great things to happen for you and your family this year. Whatever you want God to do for you, write it down and make it plain to Him and watch Him perform it before the year is out. If He said it, then you can believe it to come to past. Instead of naming that tune, name those blessings that you want to take place this year. Enjoy your wonderful Worshipping, Winning, Walking In His Purpose Wednesday!

Time of Reflections

January 2

When you are about to post something good the enemy throws a hindering block. Thank God for my phone. God is my protection, God is, He is my joy in times of sorrow, and God is, He is my all and all just to sum it up today. Give God your best and greatest praise on today. He is whatever you need him to be and more!

Time of Reflections

January 3

It's another day's journey and I am glad about it. It is a Faithful to believe, Following After Him Friday. God is so good. I give him the glory for all that He is doing and has done. I expect nothing less but a great and wonderful day. KNOW that I am praying for my family and friends that God will bless you beyond measures and that He will do exceedingly above what we can ask or think on this day! Your miracle is around the corner. The key of releasing your miracle is to PRAISE GOD despite what you are in right now. I am Convinced That You Can Praise Your Blessing Out of Heaven. Let everyone that has breath praise GOD this day and Shake Heaven and allow His Blessings to flow down in our lives. Keep Total Praise & Deliverance in your prayers. God bless you all.

Time of Reflections

____

____

____

____

____

January 4

If it had not been for the Lord on my side on this Super Saturday! Yes, this is the day in which all the working people look forward to know that they are able to have this day off. Just thanking God for what He is going to do for you this day and the days to come. Yes, I will praise Him in Advance. People were laughing they knew my pain but God will take them away. So look at me now. I don't look like what I been through. But My God, a Giant Over Disasters always make away for me. What disaster do you have that you are faced with on this day? Give it to God and allow him to work everything out just for you.

Time of Reflections

____

____

____

____

____

January 5

"How great is our GOD?" Someone sing with me How Great Is Our God! Yes, He is great and greatly to be praised from the rising of the sun until the going down of the same. He is worthy to be praised. I can feel that today is going to be an awesome day! I release it in the atmosphere right now in Jesus Name . . . . IT IS SO for both you and I. Let us get to church this day and give God all the praise that is due to him on this singing, shouting, smiling, still holding on Sunday!

Time of Reflections

____

____

____

____

____

January 6

Calling all prayer warriors that can get a prayer through. I'm looking for a miracle!

Expect the impossible! I feel the intangible and I see the invisible! And oh the sky, the sky is the limit to what I can have . . . . SO I AM GOING TO BELIEVE IT AND RECEIVE IT TODAY! I EXPECT A MIRACLE ON TODAY. If you touched and agreed with me on this day, please let me know so I can give a praise report at the end of the day. You can't see it but I testify that your miracle is on the way as well. We are Moving Forward, Making A Difference, Miracle Happening Monday.

Time of Reflections

____

____

____

____

____

January 7

Looking for a prosperous day, God is great and greatly to be praise on this Testifying, Thanking God, Trusting in Him Tuesday! Let us give praise to the children and what great things they are doing. It could always be the other way. Thank you all for being who you are and doing what you do for the children. They need us! So as we move through this Marvelous Monday, let us whisper a prayer on their behalf.

Time of Reflections

____

____

____

____

____

January 8

This is Worshipping Him, Winning, Working Wednesday! As we go through this day, let us put our trust in Him. The song writer pinned it so well, I will trust in the Lord, I will trust in the Lord, I will trust in the Lord until I die! So we must keep that song and those ways embedded in our hearts. Let us trust Him the more as never before. The time that we really need to trust in the Lord is now. Will you say and believe this, Lord I yet trust you?

Time of Reflections

____

____

____

____

____

January 9

What A mighty God we serve! Yes He is an awesome God! He is worthy of all praise. He can do way beyond what we can think & imagine. Yes, it is a miracle. As the song say I'm looking for a Supernatural Miracle. I do expect the impossible and I see the intangible and I see the invisible. Oh the sky is a limit to what I can have. Just Believe and Receive your Miracle on This Triumphant Thursday. Your Supernatural Miracle Is On The Way!

Time of Reflections

____

____

____

____

____

January 10

I didn't hit the share button! Wow, I am up giving God praise this morning. If someone would hold my mew, I would just go head and break out with a dance right here. I feel Great! Psalms deals with us Praising God: 1 Praise ye the LORD. Praise God in his sanctuary: Praise him in the firmament of his power. 2 Praise him for his mighty acts: praise him according to his excellent greatness. 3 Praise him with the sound of the trumpet: praise him with the psaltery and harp. 4 Praise him with the timbrel and dance: praise him with stringed instruments and organs. 5 Praise him upon the loud cymbals: praise him upon the high sounding cymbals. 6 Let everything that hath breath praise the LORD. Praise ye the LORD. Are You Going to Praise Him With Me?

Time of Reflections

____

____

____

____

____

January 11

Yes, another Super Saturday to be off From Work. I have decided to follow Jesus and there is no turning back whatsoever. Things get rough at times but I know in whom I believe. He is able to do what He says He will do. He is going to fulfill every prophecy to not only me but to you as well. Know as you go through out this day, God is able to do it just for you. Keep your hands in the masters' hands and everything will work out for your good.

Time of Reflections

____

____

____

____

____

January 12

God has a plan for your life and He is going to allow you to fulfill it on this Saving, Sanctifying, Singing Shouting, Smiling Sunday. You may not have everything that you desire and want but one thing for sure you are abundantly blessed. If you do not know how bless you are look at your hands, feet, mind, and then look at others who do not have hands to do for themselves, feet to get around, and do not have a their right mind to do for themselves. So as you go through this Saturday know that you are bless and are better off than others. Just thank God for His Grace and mercy for bringing us through.

Time of Reflections

____

____

____

____

____

January 13

I trade a life time for just one day! If you have not accepted Jesus as your Lord and Savior do so this day while the blood is running warm in your vain. Somebody did not get the opportunity to make that change but God has allowed YOU to be able to accept Him as your Lord and Savior. If you have back slid or fallen backwards, you too can accept God again and move forward. Be bless and Give Him All the Praise that is due to him! Help me lift Him up as you lifting Him up at your church I will be lifting Him up at Total Praise & Deliverance.

Time of Reflections

____

____

____

____

____

January 14

Yes, one more day to start a new work week. I hope and trust that your weekend is a great as you are. A lot of times we focus on what people think and feel about us but to me that is not important. The important fact is what does God has to say and how does He feels about me. I hope He can say, "This is my beloved Son & Daughter in whom I am well pleased with." Do that which is right and please God and stay out of trouble. Only what you do for Him is going to last in the end!

Time of Reflections

____

____

____

____

____

January 15

A Take it to Jesus, Testifying, Telling of His goodness Tuesday! I am so happy that I can cast all of my cares on Him because He careth for me. I know the Lord will fix it for you, if you hold to His hand and live by His command I know the Lord will fix it for you. So if something is broke and need fixed just give it to him, hold to his unchanging hand, and live by his command. If we abide in Him and he abide in us then we can go to him and ask what we will amay and he will do it for us. So as you move through this day, Take whatever problem or situation to Him and allow Him to fix it just for you (personally)!

Time of Reflections

January 16

Wonderful Working Power Wednesday! Yes, we are half way through another week and it will be over before you know it. I can't help but to encourage you in your situation, "Its only a test you are going through, its going to be over real soon, Keep the faith, don't give up, its only a test!" Yes, it's a test and if you do not pass or learn what God is trying to get you to then we will have another chance to do better the next time around. So my brother and sisters hang on in there, it will be all over in the morning! Any prayer request you have inbox me and I will make sure Total Praise & Deliverance will call you out by name and allow God to bless you real good.

Time of Reflections

January 17

This week is surely passing by. Oh how I just bless the Lord at all times and his praises are constantly in my mouth. Yes, it is Triumphant Thankful Thursday. I am so thankful to know that one more day this week and it will be another great and prosperous week behind us. As we go through this day, let us begin to think of the goodness of Jesus and all that He has done for us and allow our souls to cry to him this day and thank him for all that hes done for me. I just want to thank you Lord for all that you done for me! Anyone else going to help me thank and praise him this Thankful Thursday?

Time of Reflections

____

____

____

____

____

January 18

Final Friday is here! The day we all love. We try to do less as possible on this day but let us not get to caught up with the cares of our agenda this day and go without acknowledging him this day. Know that Everything is going to work out just fine. When the praises go up, the blessings come down. Help me send some praises up this day so we can look for our blessings to come down from Jerusalem. Yes, we shall wear a crown in that new Jerusalem. Oh, One day all the things we go through here will be worth it in the end. We will be able to walk the streets paved with Gold. I am excited when the times come.

Time of Reflections

____

____

____

____

____

January 19

Somebody prayed for me Saturday, they had me on their mind, they took their time and prayed for me, I am so glad they prayed, I am so glad they prayed I am so glad that somebody prayed for me. Let us just stop and take a moment to pray for someone that we know that is in need of prayer on this day. If each of us can take a moment to pray for one person then what do you think the Lord will do. If two or three touching and agreeing in my name, then I will be in the mist. God still answers prayer. Don't stop praying. Keep PUSHing (Pray Until Something Happen).

Time of Reflections

____

____

____

____

____

January 20

Singing Praises to God on this Super Spirit Filled Sunday! WE sing the praises to our King for He is the king of King. I am willing to and I give Him glory for He is the King. David said, I will enter His gates with thanksgiving in my heart, I will enter his courts with praise, I will say this is the day that the Lord has made I will rejoice in it because He has made me glad. As He makes us glad with how he blesses us, let us make Him glad through praising His Holy name. I got another Praise in my soul! So praise Him this day and know God's got a blessing with your name on it and what He has for you it is for you! Enjoy your Blessing.

Time of Reflections

____

____

____

____

____

January 21

Hold On your change is coming, Hold On don't worry about at Thing! Yes, on this marvelous Miracleous Monday God has it all in control. As we start this week, we have to be determined to hold on and don't let go. If you feel yourself slipping on the rope, tie a knot in it and wait until JESUS CHRIST come to your rescue. It is going to be alright a matter of a fact it is already alright. I will rejoice and be glad in it. The storm is almost gone so just hold on a little while longer. I hope and pray this not only get you through this day but through this week! Be bless and remember YOU MUST HOLD ON!

Time of Reflections

____

____

____

____

____

January 22

One More Time, One More Time, He allowed us to come together and see another Terrific Telling of His goodness Tuesday! What an awesome and mighty God we serve. Angels bow before Him, Heaven and earth adore Him, what a mighty God we serve. If you have not thanked him on this Day, pause right now and tell God thank you for all that He has done. Lord, I just want to say, "Thank You Lord For All That You Done For Me . . . ."

Time of Reflections

____

____

____

____

____

January 23

Worshipping, Working, Willing to do God's Will Wednesday! I tell you God is yet in the blessing business. Seem like I just feel my cup running over with blessings from on high. We always want God to do things for us but don't you think he wants us to do something for him. Yes, he does. He wants us to praise Him, show him that we love Him because the Bible says, If you love me, Keep my commandments. So as you go through this day write and keep those commands embedded in our hearts so we can show Him how much we love Him. He loved us so much that "For God so loved the world, that He gave his only begotten son that whosoever believeth in Him shall not perish but have everlasting life." John 3:16.

Time of Reflections

January 24

Its your time on this day! You have put others before you, you have applauded for others, but God is saying because of your faithfulness its your time. On this Triumphant Thursday know its your time. Your time and season has finally arrived. Now watch the blessings of God flow abundantly in your life.

Time of Reflections

January 25

If I could just hold out, unto tomorrow; I know that everything will be alright. If you can just make it through this Fantastic, Faithful to believe Friday everything will fall in place and it will be alright just for you!

Time of Reflections

January 26

I know God's been good to me, I know God's been good to me, Well, He woke me up this morning and started me on my way; I know God's been good to me. I hope and trust that each of you have a nice Super Sunny Saturday. I love to be resting and being lazy. I guess I cannot get any rest two Saturdays in a row like this. I am happy God blessed me once again with a big unexpected blessing I was looking for premade programs to run for tomorrow open an envelope and found $$$$$$$ . . . .

Time of Reflections

January 27

Its SUNDAY MORNNG, ITS SUNDAY MORNING! Let's get up with praises on our lips and giving him thanks. Everyday is the day to give him thanks but let us start this week by giving God some extra Thanks and Praises. I know we cannot thank him for all that he has done for us. Let us raise our praise toward him. He is so wonderful, so great, oh so worthy, loveable, my provider, my healer, my way maker, my quicker picker up, and to sum it all up he is my all and all. Facebook let us go to God's house this day and let us have some down right country time church like they did in the old days, sing the first song and the spirit would just take over. God is yet in the blessing business. When the praises go up then the blessings come down. My, My, My, don't get me started this morning. Oh God is so good awesome and worthy of the all the praises. Let's have church from the choir stand to the door, let's have church. Shake off tiredness and everything else we have to shake off and let us praise God on this smiling, singing, shouting, sensational, super Holy Ghost Sunday! What another full day for me, it is going to slow up after while but until then I MUST KEEP GOING AND GOING! Blessings fall on you all this day whoever reads it. Get yours today!

Time of Reflections

____

____

____

____

____

January 28

I have been saved all day and I am glad. I yet say by his stipes we are HEALED! Go run and tell that . . . .

Time of Reflections

____

____

____

____

____

January 29

GOD IS A MIRACLE WORKER! In what ways have He worked miracles out for you?

Time of Reflections

January 30

Lord I love you. Bless everyone this Wonderful Wednesday especially the person that reads this. The joy of the Lord is my strength.

Time of Reflections

January 31

I'm walking in the favor of God! As this month closes out on this Triumphant Thursday. I give God Almighty the praise that is due to Him. He brought us in this year and now he has allowed us to get through one month. I lift Him up on this day for just seeing one full month in another year. God is not through blessing us!

Time of Reflections

Month Two

FEBRUARY

February 1

"LORD, I JUST WANT TO THANK YOU!" Yes, ONCE AGAIN FOR BEING SO, SO, SO GOOD TO ME! Yes, one month has gone and now we are into another month. I must tell of your goodness and how you never ever failed me! If your God is not working for you after reading this book, Please try mine. He is all of that and more.! Enjoy your Faithful to believe, Following after Him, Forever in love with him Friday!

Time of Reflections

February 2

"I love you Jesus, I worship and adore you, Just want to tell you that I love you more than anything." God bless you all on this Super Saturday! Saturday is here! This is a day to rest and relax while thinking on his goodness and all that he has done for me. It's good to get in a quiet place and reflect on what God has done. Every time I turn around the Lord is blessing me. God loves you this day, His love never changes. When you wonder or are in doubt about his love for you, the think about Calvary's Cross where He died for both you and I. Unconditional Love for all people . . . . God bless you and do not forget to go to church somewhere this first Sunday in February.

Time of Reflections

February 3

"Come By Here My Lord, Come By Here! Oh Lord, Come By Here!" Now is a needed time for you to come by here. Let's go have church from the Choir stand to the door, let the praises ring, clap your hands, stomp your feet, and shout Hallelujah while dancing to the beat . . . . I pray that everyone is well on this Sunny, Smiling, Sensational Sunday Morning. I pray right now that you will bless my family, friends, love ones, and TP &D Church Family. I pray for all those who I cannot call by name and their families until you have reached everyone in the world. I just thank you for never giving up on me or counting me out. When man and other people count us out; God you always have away to count me in. For this I love and appreciate you so much. Keep Blessing me as I forever stay in your Will!

Time of Reflections

February 4

Lord, I just want to thank you for how you just allowed me to rest in you last night. I got the rest I really needed in order to jump start this full work week. Thank you for your anointing, healing power, and you just being God! I hope and trust that as we start this Monday, let us embrace it with a positive attitude and know that nothing is going to happen this week that you and GOD cannot handle. When the devil comes your way, kick him into the next day (the spirit) no individuals. Know that they are coming to attack the God in you. SO endure hardness as a good soldier and just count it all joy that God has chosen you to suffer for Him. If you suffer for Him then you will be able to reign with Him! Have a marvelous Miracle working Monday. Yes, the sky is the limit to what we can have. God is still working Miracles . . . .

Time of Reflections

February 5

Thanking God, Trusting in him, Testifying of his goodness Tuesday! God is preparing us for our Greater. Sometimes we think about what others have and wonder when our time is going to hit. Well, today I want you to know focus on you and allow God to bless you with the greater. For the Bible said, some planteth and some water but it is God who gives the increase. So remember your GREATER is on the way. It's not what it looks like. Be forever bless!

Time of Reflections

____

____

____

____

____

February 6

Yes, another halfway point we have reached. I am so thankful on this worshipping, winning, working toward my Purpose wonderful Wednesday. In this life we are going to have some ups and down. But even when we have some downs know that Jesus will pick us up every time. We just have to whisper and say Lord, help me up this day. Our good days out weighs our bad days so instead of complaining just be grateful that things are well as they are because they could be a whole lot worst. Whatever state you are in be content.

Time of Reflections

____

____

____

____

____

February 7

You are not responsible how that person treats you but you are responsible of how you treat others. Make sure the way that you are treating others that you do not mind being treated that way. If you are treating people the way we want to be treated then let us do good to everyone. There are times we have to love the devil out of a person. I am so thankful that I know that God will make your enemies your footstool. That's why I do not mind loving my enemies and haters! We must love because God is Love. Love someone on this Triumphant Thursday. Love is an action word so tell them, show them, and live it to them. What the World Needs Now Is Love Sweet Love, That's the Only Thing!

Time of Reflections

____

____

____

____

____

February 8

When things are not flourishing in my life the way I think they should, then what do I need to do. Pray about it, ask God to help and give you the increase in the area in which you desire it to take place. Keep on living because the sun is going to shine again. It won't always be like this! Yes, my brothers and sisters He (GOD) is Turning it Around for You! Expect that turn around on this Fantastic Friday as we come to a close of another work week. God is up to something great on your behalf.

Time of Reflections

____

____

____

____

____

February 9

Super Saturday has finally arrived. Let us enjoy this beautiful day. This is your day if you feel like you want to relax and sleep in a little late then do so. You have worked all week and at the end of the week some of you all have received a pay check. So with that in mind, know that we all must put our time in because payday is coming afterwhile. The race is not given to the swift or to the strong but to the one that endure to the end. I am determined to reach the end what about you! Make up in your mind that you will get to the finishing line. God bless you dearly!

Time of Reflections

February 10

God is blessing me right now oh right now, He woke me up this morning and He started me on my way, The Lord, ord, ord is blessing me Right Now. Please allow Him to bless you this day as well. Another Sunday to give praise and thanks to the our God! There is no one like our God! You can search far and wide but you will never find no one to do you like Jesus.

Time of Reflections

February 11

A marvelous, moving forward, miracles in place Monday! And Satan said unto Him, all these things will I give thee, if thou wilt fall down and worship me. Then saith Jesus unto him, get thee hence, Satan: for it is written, thou shalt worship the Lord they God, and him only shalt thou serve. Matthew 4:9-10. When the devil or the enemy offer you something that may seems good to you but not good for you, then you have to know the difference and move forward. The enemy wants you to stop praising and loving God but we have to be more determined do not let materialistic things stand in our way of our true worship.

Time of Reflections

February 12

Trusting in him, Telling of his goodness, Terrific Tuesday! Matthew 5:11, Blessed are ye, when men shall revile you, and persecute you, and shall say all manner of evil against you falsely, for my sake. We are going to be talked about criticized and everything else but we must keep focused on Jesus. I have learned what others say about you that's not good or negative let it be a lie but you keep pressing and pushing to the purpose God has for your life. Sticks and stones may break our bones and there are times names and words do hurt but we have to yet pray and seek the face of God and He will help us no matter what. The more you talk about me, the more I am going to bend my knees.

Time of Reflections

February 13

Wonderful, Worshipping, Winning Working Wednesday! Hold up the Light, Hold Up the Light for ye heaven bound soldiers, hold up the light, hold up the light, let your light shine round the world. That is what we have to do is Hold up the Light so our light can shine before men so they may see our good works and glorify the Father which is in heaven. Do not hide your light or allow it to go out. Matthew 5:14-16 says "Ye are the light of the world. A city that is set on an hill cannot be hid. Neither do men light a candle, and put it under a bushel, but on a candlestick; and it giveth light unto all that are in the house. Have a blessing and light shining day!

Time of Reflections

____

____

____

____

____

February 14

Love, Triumphant Thursday! What do you want? Sometimes we can want things so bad until it causes us to lose out with God. What is it that we want so bad that it will cause our soul to be lost in hell. I have learned do not want anything or love anything so bad that it will cause you to miss the city called HEAVEN. Some things are not worth holding on to; so whatever it is that you want so bad let it go. Once you let it go then you can move forward on this Christian Journey. Sometimes God will allow us to get what we want but lose what we had. Don't lose what you have with God. Make sure you tell someone that you love them on this Valentine's Day!

Time of Reflections

____

____

____

____

____

February 15

Fresh anointing, Feeling Good, Following him Fantastic Friday! We will tell it or die. Matthew 6:3-5 says but when thou doest alms, let not thy left hand know what thy right hand doeth: that thine alms may be in secret: and they Father which seeth in secret himself shall reward thee openly. When you bless others know that God always have a blessing for you in return. But if you make it know to what you have done, then you have already received your reward. But if you do it in secret then God will bless you openly and others will know that you are bless. So next time you bless someone, keep it between you and them unless they tell it. God bless you for wanting to help and give to someone this day.

Time of Reflections

February 16

If you do not know how to pray, then ask God to teach you what to pray and how to pray and He will do just that. Sometimes our prayers are not been answered because we pray amist, or do not supply the faith knowing that He is going to do it. When we pray ask and believe that it will come to past. The prayer that Jesus taught his disciples was: Our Father which art in heaven, Hallowed be thy name. Thy kingdom come. They will be done in earth, as it is in heaven. Give us this day our daily bread. And forgive us our debts, as we forgive our debtors. And lead us not into temptation, but deliver us from evil: For thine is the kingdom, and the power and the glory, forever. Amen. Say this prayer and it will cover every aspect of life situations that need to be handled. Keep praying God is closer than you think my sisters and brothers!

Time of Reflections

February 17

We cannot judge a book by its cover. We cannot judge people based on what they look like or what someone else told us about them. Get to know people for yourself and allow the spirit of God to give you discernment so you will know who and not to associate with. Some people may not mean us any good. For Matthew 7:1 says Judge not, that ye be not judged. So when you judge others someone is judging you. Let us go through this day without judging or passing judgment on anyone. God bless you.

Time of Reflections

____

____

____

____

____

February 18

What have you asked God for? Matthew 8:2, And, behold, there came a leper and worshipped him, saying, Lord, if thou wilt, thou canst make me clean. Allow God to make you clean and whole this day. He is willing, able, and capable of doing so. Its not the big things all the times or materialistic things we want us in life. Even through this salvation is provided. If there is any sick among you, call for the elders of the church and they shall lay hands on you, and ye shall recover and if there is any sin among you it shall be forgiven. Salvation comes through healing. God sent his word and it healed thee. Allow God to heal you this day from any physical, mental, hurt, diseases and etc. The potter wants to put you back together again. He wants to mend whatever has been broken in your life. Allow Him to do it for you this day.

Time of Reflections

____

____

____

____

____

February 19

Trusting in him, Telling of his goodness, Terrific Tuesday! Psalms 1:1-6 Blessed is the man that walketh not in the counsel of the ungodly, nor standeth in the way of sinners, nor sitteth in the seat of the scornful. But his delight is in the law of the Lord; and in his law doth he meditate day and night. And he shall be like a tree planted by the rivers of water, that bringeth forth his fruit in his season; his leaf also shall not wither; and whatsoever he doeth shall prosper. The ungodly are not so: but are like the chaff which the wind driveth away. Therefore the ungodly shall not stand in the judgment, nor sinners in the congregation of the righteous. For the Lord knoweth the way of the righteous: but the way of the ungodly shall perish.

Time of Reflections

____

____

____

____

____

February 20

Walking in the light, Worthy is the Lamb, Willing to do his will, Working, Worshipping, Wonderful Wednesday! Lord, this day "Let the words of my mouth and the meditation of my heart be acceptable in thy sight, oh Lord my strength and my redeemer" Amen! Psalm 19:14. Let us meditate on the good things of what God is getting ready to do for us!

Time of Reflections

____

____

____

____

____

February 21

Triumphant, To close to turn around Thursday! Psalms 7:1. O Lord my god, in thee do I put my trust: Save me from all them that persecute me, and deliver me. No weapon that is formed against shall prosper it wont work. God will do what He said he will do, He will stand by his Word. So what are you worried about on this day. This is the day the Lord has made my brothers and sisters rejoice and be glad in it this day. Don't worry be happy.

Time of Reflections

____

____

____

____

____

February 22

Flood gate opening, Following after God, Flowing the blessings in Fantastic Friday! Psalms 8:1. Oh Lord our Lord, How excellent is thy name in all the earth! Who hast set they glory above the heavens. There is none like you. Nobody can do us like Jesus. You can search here and there but you will never ever find nobody to do you like Him. I mean nobody can do you like Jesus, He is my Friend! This day and every day.

Time of Reflections

____

____

____

____

____

February 23

Somebody prayed for me, Seeking more after God, Still holding on Saturday! Psalms 14:1 The fool hath said in his heart, There is no God. They are corrupt, they have done abominable works, there is none that doeth good. There is A God somewhere. I never would have made it without him. He allowed me to get where I am as of today. When Elisha had to call on God, when he had to wet the altar and begin to pray and ask God to send down fire and God showed up and showed out. I too can witness that there is a God and I really do believe there is a heaven somewhere. God word is true and we must stand on His Word no matter what. A s you go through this day be more determined to stand on God's Word!

Time of Reflections

____

____

____

____

____

February 24

Sunday Morning! Sunday Morning! Yes, we know we can praise God every day. But this day we have chose to Sing, Shout, Smile, Show nough Praise him Sunday! Psalms 18:2 The Lord is my rock, and my fortress, and my deliverer; my God, my strength, in whom I will trust; my buckler, and the horn of my salvation, and my high tower. On Christ the solid rock I stand all other ground is sinking sand. So make sure we are standing and gripped to the rock. Have yourself a praise day out of this world.

Time of Reflections

____

____

____

____

____

February 25

Moving Forward, Must Make It, Marvelous Monday! Psalms 23: The Lord is my shepherd; I shall not want. He maketh me to lie down in green pastures: he leadeth me beside the still waters. He restoreth my soul: he leadeth me in the paths of righteousness for his name's sake. Yea, though I walk through the valley of the shadow of death, I will fear no evil: for thou art with me; they rod and they staff they comfort me. Thou preparest a table before me in the presence of mine enemies: thou anointest my head with oil; my cup runneth over. Surely goodness and mercy shall follow me all the days of my life: and I will dwell in the house of the Lord forever. Just know that he is our shepherd and he will supply all what we ever need.

Time of Reflections

____

____

____

____

____

February 26

Thanking God, Telling that, Trusting in him, Tuesday! Psalms 24:1-3,7-10. The earth is the Lord's and the fullness thereof; the world, and they that dwell therein. For he hath founded it upon the seas, and established it upon the floods. Who shall ascend into the hill of the Lord? Or who shall stand in his holy place. Lift up your heads, O ye gates; and be ye lift up, ye everlasting doors and the King of glory shall come in. Who is this King of Glory? The Lord strong and mighty, the Lord mighty in battle. Lift up your heads, O ye gates; even lift them up, ye everlasting doors; and the King of glory shall come in. Who is this King of glory? The Lord of hosts, he is the king of Glory. Selah. Lord, thank you for allowing me to see another Birthday and give you glory knowing that the earth is yours and everything that's in it! You are so wonderful.

Time of Reflections

____

____

____

____

____

February 27

Waiting on Him, Walking in the Light, Worshipping, Winning, Want turn back Wednesday! Psalms 27:13-14. I had fainted, unless I had believed to see the goodness of the Lord in the land of the living. Wait on the Lord: be of good courage, and he shall strengthen thine heart: wait, I say, on the Lord. Good things still come to those who wait!

Time of Reflections

___

February 28

Triumphant, That's Mine, Too Close to Turn around Thursday! Psalms 30:5-6 For his anger endureth but a moment; in his favour is life: weeping may endure for a night, but joy cometh in the morning. And in my prosperity I said, I shall never be moved. Wake up, your morning is here and what are you going to do about it. I will bless the Lord at all times and his praises shall continually be in my mouth. I praise you for my morning. I love you Lord!

Time of Reflections

Month Three

MARCH

March 1

Fill my cup, Fret not because of evil doers, Feeling Great Fantastic Friday! Psalm 30:11 thou hast turned for me my mourning into dancing: thou hast put off my sackcloth, and girded me with gladness; to the end that my glory may sing praise to thee, and not to be silent, O Lord my God, I will give thanks unto thee forever. Well, stop crying and mourning and give God praise that is due to him. I am not going to wait until the battle is over but I am going to dance now knowing that I have victory through the blood of Jesus Christ. Well, you can dance your way out of the middle of your storm!

Time of Reflections

____

____

____

____

____

March 2

Sometimes we have to encourage ourselves. We look for others to pat us on our back or be validated if we done something great but Psalms 31:24 Be of good courage, and he shall strengthen your heart, all ye that hope in the lord. Continue to be encouraged on this Super Strong, Strengthen us Saturday!

Time of Reflections

____

____

____

____

____

March 3

Sunday! Sunday! Its here and now what you are going to do about. Yes, I am going to church to worship Jesus Christ our Lord! Everything get out of my way this day and every day. I have a David attitude this morning in Psalms 34:1&3 I will bless the Lord at all times: his praise shall continually be in my mouth. O magnify the Lord with me, and let us exalt his name together. Sound like to me, there is a Holy Ghost party going on somewhere all roads leads to 211 it will take you there to Total Praise & Deliverance.

Time of Reflections

____

____

____

____

____

March 4

Moving Forward, Miracles in Progress, Marvelous Monday! Psalms 34:8 O taste and see that the Lord is good: blessed is the man that trusts in him. There are things we have to do and David gave us that command we he said, "O Taste and See that the Lord is Good!" Once we really know how good he is we want more of him. As the song writer pinned it More of You and Less of Me. It is yet well because we want him to make and mold us into what he wants us to be.

Time of Reflections

____

____

____

____

____

March 5

Trust and Never Doubt, Turning It Around, Terrific Tuesday! Psalms 37:1-5. Fret not thyself because of evildoers, neither be thou envious against the workers of iniquity. For they shall soon be cut down like the grass, and wither as the green herb. Trust in the Lord, and do good; so shall thou dwell in the land, and verily thou shalt be fed. Delight thyself also in the Lord; and he shall give thee the desires of thine heart. Commit they way unto the Lord; trust also in him; and he shall bring it to pass. Don't worry about what people say or do concerning you because in the end we are not responsible how they treat us but how we treat them. Let us show and give the love that God wants us to give. I give you a new commandment that you love one another!

Time of Reflections

____

____

____

____

____

March 6

Wash me over again, working for Jesus and I got to go through Wednesday! Psalms 37:25-26. I have been young, and now am old; yet have I not seen the righteous forsaken, nor his seed begging bread. He is ever merciful, and lendeth; and his seed is blessed. God is not going to sit in glory and hear his children cry without coming to see about us. We are his children and he is going to make sure we are doing well. Enjoy your day as he provides for us.

Time of Reflections

____

____

____

____

____

March 7

Taking it to Jesus, Telling of his Goodness, Triumphant Thursday! Psalms 39:1 I said, I will take heed to my ways, that I sin not with my tongue: I will keep my mouth with a bridle, while the wicked is before me. When we want to just say it because it pops up in our mind to say, that does not make it right. We all need to tell the Lord to put a bridle on our tongue and give us wisdom of what to say, when to say, and how to say it! There is a right way to do anything!

Time of Reflections

____

____

____

____

____

March 8

Follow Jesus, Feeling good, Faithful is our God Friday! Psalms 40:1-3. I waited patiently for the Lord; and he inclined unto me, and heard my cry. He brought me up also out of an horrible pit, out of the miry clay, and set my feet upon a rock and established my goings. And he hath put a new song in my mouth, even praise unto our God; many shall see it, and fear, and shall trust in the Lord. The Lord is a deliverer and whatever deliverance you need to day, allow him to bring you up out of the horrible pit, the miry clay and establish your goings! He is that kind of God! A strong deliverer in him will I trust.

Time of Reflections

____

____

____

____

____

March 9

Happy Anniversary to me! Yes, March 9, 1997 preached my first initial sermon. "Where do we go from Here!" This makes 17 years of preaching the Gospel. Can't wait for my 20th Anniversary. Yes, I have something forward to look to. Psalms 41:1-2. Blessed is he that considereth the poor: the Lord will deliver him in time of trouble. The Lord will preserve him, and keep him alive; and he shall be blessed upon the earth: and thou wilt not deliver him unto the will of his enemies. The Lord will strengthen him upon the bed of languishing: thou wilt make all his bed in sickness. I said, Lord, be merciful unto me: heal my soul; for I have sinned against thee. God is yet in the healing business so keep the faith and walk in your healing on this Super Smiling, Singing, Shouting, Saying Yes, to his will Sunday!

Time of Reflections

March 10

Merciful, Moving Forward, Made Up Mind Monday! Psalms 41:10-11. But thou, O Lord, be merciful unto me, and raise me up, that I may requite them. By this I know that thou favourest me, because mine enemy doth not triumph over me. Thank God for his divine favor over my life. When the favor of God is on your life what the devil says no to; God can and will say YES!

Time of Reflections

March 11

Trusting, Thanking him, Tell it like it is Terrific Tuesday! I have something to praise the Lord for! GOD is great and greatly to be praise . . . . Help me lift Him up, Help me lift Him up, Help me Lift Him Up . . . . Out of all the prayers I prayed, God yet and still answers prayer . . . .

Time of Reflections

____

____

____

____

____

March 12

The Lord is my light and my salvation on this worshipping, willing to follow Jesus all the way, winning, working for the Master Wednesday! So whom shall I fear. Do not fear what man can do to the body, but be concern about who can destroy both the body and the soul. You have a soul to be saved or lost.

Time of Reflections

____

____

____

____

____

March 13

There will be mountains that we all have to climb and there will be battles that we will have to fight but victory or defeat it's up to us to decide how can we expect to win if we never tried. Psalm 44:8. In God we boast all the day long and praise thy name for ever. So we have bragging rights to tell what good things the Lord has done for us! Have yourself a triumphant Thursday!

Time of Reflections

____

____

____

____

____

March 14

Feeling mighty happy, feeling mighty fine Yes, I am enjoying Jesus on this Fantastic Friday! Psalm 46:1. God is our refuge and strength, a very present help in trouble. Jesus Is our help in time of trouble and he will be there when no one else is.

Time of Reflections

____

____

____

____

____

March 15

Yes, its finally the weekend. Let us enjoy this Super Saturday in which the Lord has made! Psalm 48:1 Great is the Lord, and greatly to be praised in the city of our God, in the mountain of his holiness. God is great and greatly to be praise that is why I will continue to bless his name for the things he has done for me.

Time of Reflections

March 16

On this Sunny, Spirit Filled, Singing and Shouting Sunday allow God to fill us up again! Psalm 51:7,10-12. Purge me with hyssop, and I shall be clean: wash me, and I shall be whiter than snow. Create in me a clean heart, O God; and renew a right spirit within me. Restore unto me the joy of thy salvation; and uphold me with thy free spirit. What can wash away my sin nothing but the blood of Jesus!

Time of Reflections

March 17

Another Day's Journey as we Move Forward this Marvelous Monday! Psalm 55:12-13. For it was not an enemy that reproached me; then I could have borne it: neither was it he that hated me that did magnify himself against me; then I would have hid myself from him: But it was thou, a man mine equal, my guide, and mine acquaintance.

Time of Reflections

____

____

____

____

____

March 18

Turning it around Thanking God, Trusting in Him Tuesday! The Holy Spirit woke me up this morning. With songs from VaShawn Mitchell all in my head, then the Lord just had to me call out names and intercede on your behalf. God is doing great and mighty things. It was about 12:20 or 1:20 as we say, Late in the Midnight Hour He is going to turn it around. While you were sleeping God had someone praying for you . . . . What an awesome God we serve. When I got up this am to post of course the internet didn't want me to get on to tell somebody, Somebody was praying for you, they had you on their mind and they took the time to pray for you and I am so glad God allowed me to pray for you and on your behalf. But the devil messed up by allowing me to get on this afternoon . . . . God is yet doing great and mighty things. If you don't believe it just look around . . . . I hope and trust every one is trying to get themselves together due to be in the presence of the Holy Spirit!

Time of Reflections

____

____

____

____

____

March 19

"Well Done" is what I long to hear my savior say, Work while it is day because night cometh and no man can work, Walking in authority Wednesday! Psalm 55:22. Cast thy burden upon the Lord, and he shall sustain thee: he shall never suffer the righteous to be moved. Jesus he knows how much we can bare! Get rid of whatever we need to get rid of by casting it upon the Lord because he careth for us.

Time of Reflections

____

____

____

____

____

March 20

Triumphant Thursday! Psalm 56:4. In God I will praise his word, in God I have put my trust; I will not fear what flesh can do unto me. We must do what this five letter word tells us; TRUST. We must trust in the Lord that is the only way that we can make it. If we do not trust in him, then we are doomed to be lost.

Time of Reflections

____

____

____

____

____

March 21

Fantastic, Following and Fulfilling his mission for our life Friday! Psalm 57:9-11. I will praise thee, O Lord, among the people: I will sing unto thee among the nations. For thy mercy is great unto the heavens, and thy truth unto the clouds. Be thou exalted, O God, above the heavens: let thy glory be above all the earth. Yes, his grace and mercy is what brought us up to where we are now and it will continue to take us on to the end of the race.

Time of Reflections

____

____

____

____

____

March 22

Step by Step, Searching and shining the Light on my soul Saturday! Psalm 59:9. Because of his strength will I wait upon thee: for God is my defence. Don't worry about a thing. God has us covered no matter what the situation looks like right now because the sun is peeping through the clouds so the storm is almost gone. The joy of the Lord is our strength. All our help comes from the Lord and we can find strength in every situation if we just trust in the Lord and wait on him.

Time of Reflections

____

____

____

____

____

March 23

It's Another shower your blessings down on us Super, singing, Shouting, Saying Yes to his will Sunday! Psalm 61:3-4. For thou has been a shelter for me, and a strong tower from the enemy. I will abide in thy tabernacle for ever: I will trust in the covert of thy wings. I am going to hide behind the mountain where the chilly wind don't blow. Jesus is the mountain and he is our shelter in time of a storm. We can run to him and find refuge in our Father's house.

Time of Reflections

March 24

Moving Forward to Advance the Kingdom of God as we Fulfill our Purpose Monday! Psalm 62:1-2. Truly my soul waiteth upon God: from him cometh my salvation. He only is my rock and my salvation; he is my defense; I shall not be greatly moved. God is my rock. He is the rock of my salvation. Where do you go when there is no one else to turn to we can go to the rock of our salvation!

Time of Reflections

March 25

Thanking God for another Terrific, Trusting in Him, Turning it Around Tuesday! Psalm 62:5,8. My soul, wait thou only upon God; for my expectation is from him. Trust in him at all times; ye people, pour out your heart before him: God is a refuge for us. Selah.

Time of Reflections

____

____

____

____

____

March 26

I made it THANK YOU JESUS on this Wonderful Worshipping Walking in his Divine Purpose, Want turn back Wednesday! In all things give thanks because he is yet turning it around for you.

Time of Reflections

____

____

____

____

____

March 27

Triumphant Thursday! Yes we are almost at the end of another work week. We can still make noises for God bring us to the close of this week. Psalm 66:1-2 says it best, "Make a joyful noise unto God, all ye lands: Sing forth the honour of his name and make his praise glorious."

Time of Reflections

____

____

____

____

____

March 28

Following God, Feel the Breaking of Day Fantastic Friday! Psalm 67:1-3. God be merciful unto us, and bless us; and cause his face to shine upon us; Selah. That thy way may be known upon earth, thy saving health among all nations. Let the people praise thee, O god; let all the people praise thee.

Time of Reflections

____

____

____

____

____

March 29

Stay Silent Saturday and allow the Lord to speak and fight for you. Vengeance is mine saith the Lord! Lord you are good and your mercy endureth forever! I give you praise and glory for this is the day in which you have made I will rejoice and be glad in it. Yes, it is Fantastic Friday and we just need to sound off our praises this day for what He did for us on Calvary's Cross but most of all HE GOT UP with all POWER IN HIS HANDS . . . . God bless each of you and I love you all this day and everyday . . . .

Time of Reflections

____

____

____

____

____

March 30

Sunday Deliverance! Allow the Lord to deliver each of us this day. There is nothing too hard for God he hears us the first time we call. Psalm 69:16-18. Hear me, O Lord; for thy loving kindness is good: turn unto me according to the multitude of thy tender mercies. And hide not thy face from thy servant; for I am in trouble: hear me speedily. Draw nigh unto my soul, and redeem it: deliver me because of mine enemies.

Time of Reflections

____

____

____

____

____

March 31

Moving Forward Monday from the last day of this month into a new month! Psalm 70. Make haste, O God, to deliver me; make haste to help me, O Lord. Let them be ashamed and confounded that seek after my soul: let them be turned backward, and put to confusion, that desire my hurt. Let them be turned back for a reward of their shame that say, Aha, aha. Let all those that seek thee rejoice and be glad in thee: and let such as love thy salvation say continually, Let God be magnified. But I am poor and needy: make haste unto me, O God: thou art my help and my deliverer; O Lord, make no tarrying. I need you now on this day. Please come see about your children everywhere. All our help and hope lies in you!

Time of Reflections

Month Four

APRIL

April 1

Testing Your Faith, Tried by the Fire Tuesday! Psalm 71:4-5. Deliver me, O my God, out of the hand of the wicked, out of the hand of the unrighteous and cruel man. For thou art my hope, O Lord God: thou are my trust from my youth. Keep your trust in the Lord! All of our help is in the Lord.

Time of Reflections

____

____

____

____

____

April 2

Wonderful, Working for Jesus Wednesday! Psalm 75:1. Unto thee, O God, do we give thanks, unto thee do we give thanks: for that thy name is near thy wondrous works declare. He is worthy of all the praises that we can give him and more. He has done great things for us all, so bless his Holy Name.

Time of Reflections

____

____

____

____

____

April 3

Try Jesus, Turning it Around Thursday! Psalm 77:11-12. I will remember the works of the Lord: surely I will remember thy wonders of old. I will meditate also of all thy work, and talk of thy doings. Try Jesus and you will find out that he is alright and that he will turn your situation around. We must meditate on his goodness and share it with others.

Time of Reflections

____

____

____

____

____

April 4

Following Jesus, Fantastic, Faithful to believe Friday! Psalm 84:4-5. People wonder if they should go to church and praise the Lord. You can praise him wherever you choose to but Blessed are they that dwell in thy house: they will be still praising thee. Selah. Blessed is the man whose strength is in thee; in whose heart are the ways of them.

Time of Reflections

____

____

____

____

____

April 5

Saying Yes to His Will Saturday! Do not fall into the hands of an angry God. God he is just. Psalm 85:2-4. Thou hast forgiven iniquity of thy people; thou hast covered all their sin. Selah. Thou hast taken away all thy wrath: thou hast turned thyself from the fierceness of thine anger. Turn us, O God of our salvation and cause thine anger toward us to cease. When we do what we are suppose to do and even at times we do not thank God for Grace & Mercy yet pleading our case.

Time of Reflections

____

____

____

____

____

April 6

Shouting, Smiling, Standing Strong Sunday! Psalm 86:2-3. Preserve my soul; for I am holy: O thou my god, save thy servant that trusteth in thee. Be merciful unto me, O Lord: for I cry unto thee daily. We must cry out to the Lord daily. Daily I will worship thee, Lamb of God that was slain for me. Daily I, Daily I, Daily I will worship thee. Let us worship Christ the Lord this day and everyday to come.

Time of Reflections

____

____

____

____

____

April 7

Moving Forward Marvelous, Miracles happening Monday! Psalms 86:15. But thou, O Lord, are a God full of compassion, and gracious, longsuffering, and plenteous in mercy and truth. We need to be kind one to another. We need to show compassion toward our brothers and sisters. God is love and we are in him and he is in us then we can't help but show the Love for our fellow man.

Time of Reflections

April 8

Trusting in Him, Terrific Tuesday! Psalm 88:2. Let my prayer come before thee: incline thine ear unto my cry. The song writer wrote, I cried and he delivered me; he delivered my pour soul. We have to cry out to the lord and we cry out and call upon his name, then he will come to our rescue.

Time of Reflections

April 9

What A Mighty God, Worshipping, Walking in His divine Purpose, Wonderful Wednesday! 4:00 am up worshipping Jesus: "He makes me happy; He makes me whole; He takes the pain away, I'm so in love with Him . . ." What an awesome worshipping experience or should I say what a good way to wake up. THANK MY PERSONAL CHOIR DIRECTOR FOR TEACHING ME THIS SONG Personally. I have to work on the second part. God is yet doing great and wonderful things. I am walking in authority living life the way it suppose to be . . . . Today is Terrific Thanking Him Tuesday for all that He has done. Take some time out of your schedule to share one thing God has done for you in the last 24 hours . . . . I thank Him for showering me with His anointing and waking me up this morning, close me in my right mind, I just want to I thank you Lord for all that you done for me. Be forever bless my family, friends, congregation, and anyone that I come in contact with. May the blessings of God maketh you rich and add no sorrow with it!

Time of Reflections

____

____

____

____

____

April 10

Triumphant, This is my story, thanking God Thursday! Psalm 90:1. Lord, thou hast been our dwelling place in all generations. The safest place for all of us is to be in the will of God. He is our shelter in time of storm. Dwell in his presence on this Triumphant Thursday.

Time of Reflections

____

____

____

____

____

April 11

Fret Not, Following After God, Fantastic, Faithful to believe Friday! Friday, Psalm 90:17. And let the beauty of the Lord our God be upon us: and establish thou the work of our hands upon us; yea, the work of our hands establish thou it. Whatever your hands find to do it, let us do it whole heartedly and with excellence for the Master.

Time of Reflections

____

____

____

____

____

April 12

Show Me how to love again, Staying in my lane Saturday! Psalm 91:1-4. He that dwelleth in the secret place of the most High shall abide under the shadow of the Almighty. I will say of the Lord, He is my refuge and my fortress: my God; in him will I trust. Surely he shall deliver thee from the snare of the fowler, and from the noisome pestilence. He shall cover thee with his feathers, and under his wings shalt thou trust: his truth shall be thy shield and buckler.

Time of Reflections

____

____

____

____

____

April 13

Somebody are to testify, super, shouting, smiling saying yes to his will Sunday! Psalm 91:9-11. Because thou hast made the Lord, which is my refuge, even the most High, thy habitation; There shall no evil befall thee, neither shall any plague come nigh thy dwelling. For he shall give his angels charge over thee, to keep thee in all thy ways. He is a keeper and he will keep you if you want to be kept. He will not force himself on you! Accept and Keep him this day!

Time of Reflections

April 14

Moving Forward, Marvelous, Miracles Happening Monday! Psalm 92:1-2. It is a good thing to give thanks unto the Lord, and to sing praises unto thy name, O most High: To shew forth thy lovingkindness in the morning, and thy faithfulness every night.

Time of Reflections

April 15

Telling of his Goodness, Testifying, Thanking Him Tuesday! Psalm 94:3-4. Lord, how long shall the wicked, how long shall the wicked triumph? How long shall they utter and speak hard things? And all the workers of iniquity boast themselves? You are not responsible how people treat you but you are responsible how you treat them. Let God take care of them.

Time of Reflections

____

____

____

____

____

April 16

It's Well, Winning, Waiting on the Lord, Worshipping him Wednesday! Psalm 95:1-2. O Come, let us sing unto the Lord: let us make a joyful noise to the rock of our salvation. Let us come before his presence with thanksgiving, and make a joyful noise unto him with psalms.

Time of Reflections

____

____

____

____

____

April 17

To God be the Glory, Trusting and Telling the devil to get behind you Thursday! Psalm 96:1-4. O sing unto the Lord a new song: sing unto the Lord, all the earth. Sing unto the Lord, bless his name; shew forth his salvation from day to day. Declare his glory among the heather, his wonders among all people. For the Lord is great, and greatly to be praised: he is to be feared above all gods.

Time of Reflections

____

____

____

____

____

April 18

Fix it Jesus, Following Him For life Friday! Psalm 96:7-9. Give unto the Lord, o ye kindreds of the people, give unto the Lord glory and strength. Give unto the Lord the glory due unto his name: bring an offering, and come into his courts. O worship the Lord in the beauty of holiness: fear before him all the earth.

Time of Reflections

____

____

____

____

____

April 19

Someday my God is going to separate the right from the wrong, Saturday! Psalm 97:9,12. For thou, Lord, art high above all the earth: thou are exalted far above all gods. Rejoice in the Lord, ye righteous; and give thanks at the remembrance of his holiness.

Time of Reflections

April 20

Sunday Morning Praise Break Time! Psalm 98:1. O sing unto the Lord a new song; for he hath done marvelous things: his right hand, and his holy arm, hath gotten him the victory. He has done get things and we are to bless his name. If the Lord has done anything for you, then you are to run and tell that! I know I am . . . .

Time of Reflections

April 21

Might as well Praise him, Moving Forward, Marvelous Monday! Psalm 99:5. Exalt ye the Lord our god, and worship at his footstool; for he is holy. Holy, Holy, Holy is our God. We have to worship Him. What a mighty God we serve, the angels bow before him heaven and earth adore him; what a mighty God we serve. It's a reminder that we serve a mighty God!

Time of Reflections

April 22

To close to turn around, Terrific, telling of his goodness Tuesday! With that in mind we might as well do as Psalm 100 says, "Make a joyful noise unto the Lord, all ye lands. Serve the Lord with gladness: come before his presence with singing. Know ye that the Lord he is God: it is he that hath made us, and not we ourselves; we are his people, and the sheep of his pasture. Enter into his gates with thanksgiving, and into his courts with praise: be thankful unto him, and bless his name. For the Lord is good; his mercy is everlasting; and his truth endureth to all generations."

Time of Reflections

April 23

Working for Jesus and I got to go through, Wonderful, Worshipping Wednesday! Psalm 102:1-2. Hear my prayer, O Lord, and let my cry come unto thee. Hide not they face from me in the day when I am in trouble; incline thine ear unto me: in the day when I call answer me speedily.

Time of Reflections

____

____

____

____

____

April 24

Turn it around, Telling Satan No, Triumphant Thursday! Psalm 103:1-5. Bless the Lord, O my soul: and all that is within me, bless his holy name. Bless the Lord, O my soul, and forget not all his benefits: Who forgiveth all thine iniquities; who healeth all thy diseases; Who redeemeth thy lfie from destruction; who crowneth thee with lovingkindness and tender mercies; who satisfieth thy mouth with good things; so that thy youth is renewed like the eagle's. Bless the Lord oh my soul and all that is within me bless his holy name. He has done great things for you and I so we must bless his holy name.

Time of Reflections

____

____

____

____

____

April 25

Faithful to believe, Following after his righteousness, standing Firm Friday! Psalm 105:1-4. O Give thanks unto the Lord call upon his name: make known his deeds among the people. Sing unto him, sing psalms unto him: talk ye of all his wondrous works. Glory ye in his holy name: let the heart of them rejoice that seek the Lord. Seek the Lord, and his strength: seek his face evermore.

Time of Reflections

____

____

____

____

____

April 26

Shaking the devil off, Super, Sensational, Serving the Lord will pay off Saturday! WHAT A HOLY GHOST TIME IN THE LORD! THANK GOD I DIDNT GET STOPPED I WAS DRIVING UNDER THE INFLUENCE OF THE HOLY GHOST . . . . GOD IS MOVING AND BLESSING HIS PEOPLE LIKE NEVER BEFORE. IT IS my prayer Lord, whatever you doing in this season please don't do it without me . . . . I want to be included. God bless you all and have a restful night this night in the Lord . . . .

Time of Reflections

____

____

____

____

____

April 27

Step Back and Let God do it, Super shouting, singing, smiling, serving God until I die Sunday! Psalm 105:15. Saying, touch not mine anointed, and do my prophets no harm. Be careful how you treat people, because if you touch and put your mouth on God's anointed you bring damnation upon your soul. Be careful little hands what you do, be careful little mouth what you say, your father up above is looking down below so be careful little hands what you do!

Time of Reflections

____

____

____

____

____

April 28

My Soul loves Jesus, Moving Forward, Marvelous, Miracle Making Monday! If God promised it to you, then it is already guaranteed. Psalm 105:39-42. He spread a cloud for a covering; and fire to give light in the night. The people asked, and he brought quails, and satisfied them with the bread of heaven. He opened the rock, and the waters gushed out; they ran in the dry places like a river. For he remembered his holy promise, and Abraham his servant. God will provide for you! He will supply all of your needs according to his riches in glory!

Time of Reflections

____

____

____

____

____

April 29

Terrific, Telling of his Goodness, Trusting in the Lord Tuesday! Psalm 106:1. Praise ye the Lord. O give thanks unto the Lord; for he is good: for his mercy endureth for ever. His mercy endureth forever. It is because of his grace and mercy that brought us through and we are living this moment because of him and we want to thank him and praise him too, your grace and mercy brought us through.

Time of Reflections

April 30

Work it out, Walk it out, Watch it out, and Wait it out Wonderful, Winning, Wednesday! Psalm 106:8-11. Nevertheless he saved them for his name's sake, that he might make his mighty power to be known. He rebuked the Red sea also, and it was dried up; so he led them through the depths, as through the wilderness. And he saved them from the hand of him that hated them, and redeemed them from the hand of the enemy. And the waters covered their enemies: there was not one of them left.

Time of Reflections

Month Five

May

May 1

Triumphant, Tremendous, Turning it Around Thursday! Psalm 107:1-2. Let the redeemed of the Lord say so, whom he hath redeemed from the hand of the enemy; and gathered them out of the lands, from the east, and from the west, from the north, and from the south.

Time of Reflections

____

____

____

____

____

May 2

Fantastic, Following Him Friday! Psalm 107:6,8. Then they cried unto the Lord in their trouble, and he delivered them out of their distresses. Oh that men would praise the Lord for his goodness, and for his wonderful works to the children of men.

Time of Reflections

____

____

____

____

____

May 3

Saying Yes to his will Saturday! Psalm 108:1. O God, my heart is fixed; I will sing and give praise, even with my glory. Sign me up for the Christians jubilee and write my name on the roll, I've been changed since the Lord has lifted me, I want to be ready when my Jesus come!

Time of Reflections

____

____

____

____

____

May 4

Sunday Morning! Let us go to the house of God and give him glory and honor that is due to him. When praises go up the blessings come down! Psalm 108:12-13. Give us help from trouble: for vain is the help of man. Through God we shall do valiantly: for he it is that shall tread down our enemies.

Time of Reflections

____

____

____

____

____

May 5

Moving Forward, Manifesting Monday! Psalm 109:26-27. Help me, O Lord my God: O save me according to thy mercy. That they may know that this is in thy hand; that thou, Lord, hast done it.

Time of Reflections

____

____

____

____

____

May 6

Trusting in him, Turning it around Tuesday! Psalm 110:1,3. The Lord said unto my Lord, Sit thou at my right hand, until I make thine enemies thy footstool. Thy people shall be willing in the day of thy power, in the beauties of holiness from the womb of the morning: thou hast the dew of thy youth.

Time of Reflections

____

____

____

____

____

May 7

Working for Jesus, Willing to go all the way Wednesday! Psalm 111:2,3. The works of the Lord are great, sought out of all them that have pleasure therein. His work is honourable and glorious: and his righteousness endureth for ever.

Time of Reflections

____

____

____

____

____

May 8

Triumphant, Taking it to Jesus Thursday! Psalm 111:10. The fear of the Lord is the beginning of wisdom: a good understanding have all they that do his commandments: his praise endureth for ever.

Time of Reflections

____

____

____

____

____

May 9

Faithful to Believe, Following him Friday! Psalm 113:1-4. Praise ye the Lord, Praise, O ye servants of the Lord, praise the name of the Lord. Blessed be the name of the Lord from this time forth and for evermore. From the rising of the sun unto the going down of the same the Lord's name is to be praised. The Lord is high above all nations, and his glory above the heavens.

Time of Reflections

____

____

____

____

____

May 10

Shaping Up, Standing Still Saturday! Psalm 115:13-15. He will bless them that fear the Lord, both small and great. The Lord shall increase you more and more, you and your children. Ye are blessed of the Lord which made heaven and earth.

Time of Reflections

____

____

____

____

____

May 11

Spirit Fall On Me, Standing on a Sure Foundation Sunday! Psalm 116:1-2. I love the Lord, because he hath heard my voice and my supplications. Because he hath inclined his ear unto me, therefore will I call upon him as long as I live. Happy Mothers' Day to each of you and I pray you all have a great and wonderful day! A special Happy Mothers' Day to all the Mothers of Total Praise & Deliverance, Mt. Zion, B.A.B.M, and The Church of God Founded By Jesus Christ as a whole. Yes, it will be happening once again at TP & D. We will be showing you how to really celebrate and salute mothers and women on this special day! God bless you dearly. Happy Mother's day to Jennie Pearl McNeill, and Pastor Alice Lee Glover you all were just incredible producing awesome children. Thank You and continue to RIP . . .

Time of Reflections

____

____

____

____

____

May 12

Moving Forward; Manifesting Monday. Yes, today marks a new day for all of us and if you have not encouraged yourself lately, then I want you to know that you are "A GREAT SOMEBODY!" Don't let anyone shatter, break, or deter your dreams. If you think you can, then you can be what you want to be and then some. We are more than conquerors through Jesus Christ that loves us.

Time of Reflections

____

____

____

____

____

May 13

Trusting in him, Turning it Around Tuesday! Psalm 116:12-14. What shall I render unto the Lord for all his benefits toward me? I will take the cup of salvation and call upon the name of the Lord. I will pay my vows unto the Lord now in the presence of all his people.

Time of Reflections

May 14

Working For Jesus, Willing to go all the way Wednesday! Psalm 117. O Praise the Lord, all ye nations: praise him, all ye people. For his merciful kindness is great toward us: and the truth of the Lord endureth for ever. Praise ye the Lord.

Time of Reflections

May 15

Triumphant, Taking it to Jesus Thursday! I love you Lord and I lift my voice to worship you, oh my soul rejoice take charge my king in what you hear and let it be a sweet sweet sound in your ear. Lord Jesus you, mean so much to me. You are my everything and I thank you even for A RIGHT NOW PRAISE FOR A RIGHT NOW CHANGE in how you are making and molding me into what you want me to be. I worship you this day for who you are. If it had not been for you on our side then where would I be at this point in my life, YOU ARE THE GREAT I AM . . . . I cannot praise and thank you enough, but this day I am going to keep putting a dent into it to let you know I appreciate you so much. Keep blessing my family, my FRIENDs, Church Families, Work Family, and everyone I come in contact with, and I would not leave you out in no form or fashion my FACEBOOK family who read my posting and are encouraged, inspired and lifted up because I listen to your voice on what to post and NO JUNK POSTING IN HERE . . . . Thank You Jesus since I accepted you, my life has no longer been the same and I know you are transitioning some things in my life and I say HAVE YOUR WAY, HAVE YOUR WAY, Have Your Way . . . .

Time of Reflections

____

____

____

____

____

May 16

Faithful to Believe, Following him Friday! Psalm 118:17-21. I shall not die, but live, and declare the works of the Lord. The Lord hath chastened me sore: but he hath not given me over unto death. Open to me the gates of righteousness: I will go into them, and I will praise the Lord: This gate of the Lord, into which the righteous shall enter. I will praise thee: for thou hast heard me, and art become my salvation.

Time of Reflections

____

____

____

____

____

May 17

Shaping Up, Standing Still Saturday! Psalm 119:2,7. Blessed are they that keep his testimonies, and that seek him with the whole heart. I will praise thee with the uprightness of heart, when I shall have learned thy righteous judgments.

Time of Reflections

May 18

Spirit Fall on Me, Standing on a Sure Foundation Sunday! Psalm 119:33-35. Teach me, O Lord, the way of thy statues; and I shall keep it unto the end. Give me understanding, and I shall keep thy law; yea, I shall observe it with my whole heart. Make me to go in the path of thy commandments; for therein do I delight.

Time of Reflections

May 19

Moving Forward, Manifesting Monday! Psalm 119:57-59. Thou art my portion, O Lord: I have said that I would keep thy words. I entreated thy favor with my whole heart: be merciful unto me according to thy word. I thought on my ways, and turned my feet unto thy testimonies.

Time of Reflections

____

____

____

____

____

May 20

Trusting in him, Turning it Around Tuesday! Psalm 119:66-68. Teach me good judgment and knowledge: for I have believed thy commandments. Before I was afflicted I went astray: but now have I kept thy word. Thou art good, and doest good, teach me thy statues.

Time of Reflections

____

____

____

____

____

May 21

Working for Jesus, Willing to go all the Way Wednesday! Psalm 119:71,76-77. It is good for me that I have been afflicted; that I might learn thy statues. Let, I pray thee, thy merciful kindness be for my comfort, according to thy word unto thy servant. Let thy tender mercies come unto me, that I may live: for thy law is my delight.

Time of Reflections

____

____

____

____

____

May 22

Triumphant, Taking it to Jesus Thursday! Psalm 119:97,99. O how love I thy law! It is my meditation all the day. I have more understanding than all my teachers: for thy testimonies are my meditation.

Time of Reflections

____

____

____

____

____

May 23

Faithful to Believe, Following him Friday! Psalm 119:129,133-135. Thy testimonies are wonderful: therefore doth my soul keep them. Order my steps in thy word: and let not any iniquity have dominion over me. Deliver me from the oppression of man: so will I keep thy precepts. Make thy face to shine upon thy servant; and teach me thy statues.

Time of Reflections

____

____

____

____

____

May 24

Shaping Up, Standing Still Saturday! Psalm 119:143-145. Trouble and anguish have taken hold on me: yet thy commandments are my delights. The righteousness of thy testimonies is everlasting: give me understanding, and I shall live. I cried with my whole heart; hear me, O Lord: I will keep thy statues.

Time of Reflections

____

____

____

____

____

May 25

Hello wonderful people it is a Spirit Fall on Me, Standing on a Sure Foundation Sunday! I am believing God for a great day! God is breaking chains in every aspect of your life because there is power in the name of Jesus . . . . I hope and trust you all have a great day . . . Just in a quiet worship mood for what God is going to do. Watch God, He is moving on your behalf.

Time of Reflections

____

____

____

____

____

May 26

Moving Forward, Manifesting Monday! Psalm 119:166-168. Lord, I have hoped for thy salvation, and done thy commandments. My soul hath kept thy testimonies; and I love them exceedingly. I have kept thy precepts and thy testimonies: for all my ways are before thee.

Time of Reflections

____

____

____

____

____

May 27

Trusting in him, Turning it Around Tuesday! Psalm 119:175-176. Let my soul live, and it shall praise thee; and let thy judgments help me. I have gone astray like a lost sheep; seek thy servant; for I do not forget thy commandments.

Time of Reflections

May 28

Working for Jesus and I got to go through, Willing to go all the Way Wednesday! Psalm 120:7. I am for peace: but when I speak, they are for war.

Time of Reflections

May 29

Triumphant, Taking it to Jesus Thursday! Psalm 121. I will lift up mine eyes unto the hills, from whence cometh my help. My help cometh from the Lord, which made heaven and earth. He will not suffer thy foot to be moved: he that keepeth thee will not slumber. Behold, he that keepeth Israel shall neither slumber nor sleep. The Lord is thy keeper: the Lord is thy shade upon thy right hand. The sun shall not smite thee by day, nor the moon by night. The Lord shall preserve thee from all evil: he shall preserve thy soul. The Lord shall preserve thy going out and thy coming in from this time forth, and even for evermore.

Time of Reflections

____

____

____

____

____

May 30

Faithful to Believe, Following Him Friday! Psalm 123:3-4. Have mercy upon us, O Lord, have mercy upon us: for we are exceedingly filled with contempt. Our soul is exceedingly filled with the scorning of those that are at ease, and with the contempt of the proud.

Time of Reflections

____

____

____

____

____

May 31

Shaping Up, Standing Still Saturday! It's another day that the Lord has kept me! I am glad about it. Last night sleep was much needed and I give God the glory for just being able to rest and sleep in His presence. Yes, it's one more day before the big day gets here (SUNDAY) I am going to embrace it with Love, JOY, Peace, Favor, Emanuel, Destined for Purpose, Through It All, Determined and most of all with MY EVERYTHING. With all of this I cannot go wrong. God is Love and He is definitely my Peace and I worship Him on this day and every day. I hope and trust everyone just have a great day because this is the day the Lord has made we must rejoice and be glad in it. I will say this find one thing you are thankful for and meditate on that, knowing you have a right to praise Him because your JERICHO Wall is coming down. Your Praise and Victory Shout will make it possible! I better not start this morning but with that all said, Please let us remember to pray for the children/students who are taking the EOG test and other test on today knowing that God is going to see them through. Always remember God Loves ESPECIALLY YOU!

Time of Reflections

____

____

____

____

____

Month Six

June

June 1

Spirit Fall on Me, Standing on a Sure Foundation Sunday! It is another month that we are in, we are half way through this year. I yet say as my theme: "This is the Year of Manifestation!" Time is yet moving and it behooves us to make every step count. Yes, it's the day in which the Lord has made. I will embrace it despite what the enemy tries to bring my way. I will allow peace and happiness to abide within me. Yes, it's another day He has yet kept me and I am glad about it. I hope and trust that this will be a lovely day for all of US . . . . Just continue those in prayer that is going through the real storms and also the storms of life. God is yet able to see everyone through. Keep praying and believing.

Time of Reflections

____

____

____

____

____

June 2

Moving Forward, Manifesting Monday! I get JOY when I think about what He has done for me. God is blessing me right now oh right now, He woke me up this morning and started me on my way, ay ay ay, The Lord is blessing me right now! I Love the Lord with all that's within me. We do not know when the time will come but we have to prepare and be ready now so we want miss the journey. Allow God to touch you this day and allow His joy to fill your soul and when something happen you will know He touched you and He made you WHOLE . . . . If I could I would just let you know just how good I am feeling but this morning I don't even have the words to express it. Be bless on this Marvelous Monday Morning.

Time of Reflections

____

____

____

____

____

June 3

Trusting in him, Turning it Around Tuesday! I want each of you to know that He Will Make It Alright, Jesus Will Make It Alright. That song woke me up early this morning. So as you go through this day and the last full work week with the students know whatever comes up or arises on this day, Jesus Will Make It Alright. This is not only for educators but for everyone that Believes. God is just so great and mighty and He deserves the praises. Seem like we cannot praise Him enough for all He has done for us. But I try to put a dent in it from time to time to let Him know how much I appreciate Him. I pray you have a great, glorious, giving him praise, gotta get yours Tuesday! . . . .

Time of Reflections

____

____

____

____

____

June 4

Working for Jesus, Willing to go all the Way Wednesday! Lord, I just want to thank you because the prayers of the righteous availeth much. What a mighty God we serve. Thank God for the prayer. Lord, I slept so hard last night and slept really well. To God be the Glory. I finally started reading the Further Study in my Sunday School book, I didn't read only Monday but did Tuesday as well. Thank God for getting back in the reading flow to be prepared for Sunday School in advance. That was one thing I wanted to do different this year and God has me going. I hope and trust each of you all have a Wonder Wednesday. God loves you so much and He is always concerned about us and He is working things out according to His Plan for our lives. So step back and let God handle it. A Right Now Praise for A RIGHT NOW CHANGE . . . . Keep praising and blessing His name cause that Change is going to come . . . According to your faith be it unto you this DAY.!!!!!!!!

Time of Reflections

____

____

____

____

____

June 5

Triumphant, Taking it to Jesus Thursday! Hello, I hope and trust that each of you woke up with a Worship and Praise on Your Lips. Just reflecting on God's goodness. Let us do not forget to pray for the children who are taking their tests today or the ones will be taking them. May the blessings of God keep them calm and allow them to focus and do good. God is up to something great. Eyes haven't seen nor ears heard, neither has it enter into the heart of man what God has in store for you. But it has been revealed through His Son Jesus. Expect Your Great, Its Definitely On the Way! Bless his name on this Triumphant Thursday! Three things that excites us as educators, when school starts, when we are half way through the year and then at the end! Parents like to see it begin and hate to see it end. Just Saying. He will do it for you.

Time of Reflections

____

____

____

____

____

June 6

Following him, Faithful to believe Friday! Yes, Yes, Yes, this week is over not rushing it at all. But God knows all. Embrace this day with love, peace, joy and happiness as we bless others. God is just awesome and excellent is His name in all the Earth. Just continue to look to the hills from whence cometh your help cause all of our help comes from the Lord. We have to be determined don't let nothing or no one separate us from the Love of God. Time is winding up more today than it was on yesterday. If it presents itself to you, then God will carry you through it. The joy of the Lord is our strength. I will say rejoice and be glad in it and again I say Rejoice. Anyone going to rejoice with me on this Fantastic Friday! I am Thanking God for you in advance.

Time of Reflections

____

____

____

____

____

June 7

I will shout with a LOUD voice on this Shaping Up, Standing Still Saturday! It's almost over now through my natural eyes. ITS OVER EVEN NOW . . . . I DECLARE AND DECREE IT IN THE NAME OF JESUS. Yes, dont wait til the battle is over but we can shout right now . . . . I hope and trust everyone had a wonderful week and if not I hope and trust that this will be one of the greatest days of your life yet. Just keep praying and holding on to God's unchanging hands because he is up to something on your behalf. God bless you this day and everyday to come. Feeling Good because He makes me happy, He makes me whole, He takes the Pain away I am so in love with you (God/Jesus)! Join In. Wow, time is moving this morning.

Time of Reflections

____

____

____

____

____

June 8

Spirit Fall on me, Standing on a Sure Foundation Sunday! We must be sure and very sure that our anchor holds and grips that solid rock. That Rock is Jesus he is the one, that rock is Jesus we must be sure! The commercial says, 'Raise your hand, if you are sure!" I am sure that I am rooted and grounded in the word of God. There are higher heights and deeper depths. We will get through this once again. Enjoy the rest of your Super, beautiful Sunday!

Time of Reflections

____

____

____

____

____

June 9

Its one more day, one more step He is preparing me what's coming my way! Yes, I can add a little remix to it this morning. I am feeling good down in my soul. God just keep doing great and mighty things. Now Jesus take the wheel. I trust you Lord. I hope and trust each of you have a wonderful day as you lift up the name of Jesus may the praises of God be so high and the anointing be in the house to break every chain and pull down every strong hold against the enemy! Just Rejoice in the Lord because its already done, done. I decree and declare it no need of praying about it anymore just thank God knowing through the eyes of faith it is already worked out and its already done . . . . Do you have a RIGHT NOW PRAISE FOR A RIGHT NOW CHANGE . . . I know I do even now a 2 stepper is in order this Moving Forward; Manifesting Monday morning!

Time of Reflections

____

____

____

____

____

June 10

Trusting in Him, Turning it Around Tuesday! Lord I thank you for this day in which you have made I will rejoice and be glad in it. I like to say it like this I will bless your name, I will bless your name, I will bless your holy name! He is awesome like that when you don't see how you made it from then until now, it was nobody but GOD that brought us through. I just give him all the praise glory and the honor for all that he has done for me! I hope and trust that this will be a beautiful day for everyone. So hold on and hang on in there because A RIGHT NOW PRAISE FOR A RIGHT NOW CHANGE. WE made it this far so we all should encourage ourselves and go on a little bit further. So as you go out today, tell yourself to go a little further because there is something on the other side of through Just for you! I pray for strength right now for each of us and someone in particular that God would just shower down even now. I pray this day would jump start a new beginning of a fantastic day. I declare and decree it in Jesus Name and I speak It is so . . . .

Time of Reflections

____

____

____

____

____

June 11

Empty Me! I want more of you and less of me. Walking with me Lord and Willing to go Through Worshipping Wednesday! God is up to something really great. Prayer is yet changing things, situations, people, and things. It is the prayer of the righteous that availeth much. If you are praying, I am praying things have no choice but to get better. Your struggling is over this day, I declare and decree on your behalf just let go and let God as you release your faith so that he can do the work. According to your faith be it unto you. If you can only believe, then all things are possible. And if you know that you prayed about it, and put it in God's hands, then just pray a prayer of thanks knowing that it is already done! God is getting me to that point, pray about it once and move on to something else knowing that He's got it and he is working on it. Therefore, I will keep moving and focusing on something else as I intercede on behalf of my family, friends, love ones and even my enemies. Whatever we pray for others God will allow things to take place in our life. We reap what we sow, so as I sow prayers for you, I am reaping some blessings for myself! Be bless and have a great day . . . .

Time of Reflections

____

____

____

____

____

June 12

My God Reign, My God Reign, He reigns over every name . . . . With dominion and power my God Reign. Know this day as you go through this Triumphant, Taking it to Jesus Thursday, that God does reign!!! That is encouragement within itself. God is yet in the blessing business no matter how it looks right now just keep your hands and God hands cause in your morning time, He is turning it around for you!

Time of Reflections

____

____

____

____

____

June 13

What a mighty God we serve. Lord, I just thank you for last night oh I just felt so good from your touch. He touched me and He made me whole. Yes, I went to bed early last night and I woke up at 3am and was able to go back to sleep til 5am without any problems. It's so good to rest in the arms of Jesus. Got up did my daily reading this morning and I know without of a doubt that nothing is going to happen to me today nor you that GOD cannot handle. I decree and declare a great and wonderful day in the name of Jesus, discord and confusion we bind it up right now. We release a new attitude and a new outlook about life on this day. So walk in the newness of life. "God is doing a new thing whatever you ask for and whatever you pray for it shall not be denied," saith the Lord. Rejoice on this Following him, Faithful to Believe Friday!

Time of Reflections

____

____

____

____

____

June 14

Shaping Up, Standing Still, and Settling for the Best Saturday! Just thinking how God has yet bless me and I know that over 33 days ago He has done something for me and I haven't been the same since then. He allowed me to go on a 16 day of prayer journey and even in that time frame He has allowed people to be healed, delivered and set free. You will never be the Same Again. (I can hear WINGATE COMMUNITY SINGING THAT SONG). I cannot describe it but I can say God is incredible, and incredible God deserves incredible praise. I praise Him for allowing me to get through and bringing me through every situation and storm I encountered in life. It made me a stronger person. I will say this, "the anointing and the spirit of God that dwells in you will cost you something and WILL TELL YOU WHEN TO KEEP your mouth closed." Be blessed this Super Saturday. You know my cup is overflowing this morning I can hear the abundance of rain in my spirit. Your abundance is on the way. In the words of Pastor Glover Your Breakthrough is around the Corner!

Time of Reflections

____

____

____

____

____

June 15

Happy Father's Day to all the Fathers. I give thanks and praise to all the men that had a great influence in my life. Mr. Martin, The Late Mr. Fennell, Mr. James Johnson, Mr. Louis Thomas, Mr. Thomas Clawson, Mr. Amos Tolson. Thank You All! May heaven open up and bless you all this day and every day. Good morning Holy Spirit, I just want to thank you, thank you Jesus for this day. Yes, it is another Super Spirit Touch Me One More Time Sunday; God has allowed you and I to see and I am going to make the best of it. I am glad that he takes care of me. My soul loves Jesus, My soul loves Jesus, My soul loves Jesus Bless His name . . . . And I can go on and on with that song. Oh I bless His name if only you knew what God was doing for you or if you just peeped into your future, oh my God you would be praising Him right now. I see the plans of the enemy were denounced and done away with. But God's report and plan prevailed on my behalf. Oh God I thank you. I feel like yet going on though trials come on every hand, I feel like going on. I feel like pressing my way, oh yes, I feel like pressing my way, though trials come on every hand, I feel like pressing my way. Even with that, we got to endure hardness as a good soldier. I am blessed to know what God is yet doing for you, you and especially you. Be blessed this day as you were on yesterday but a little better today. New mercies I see every morning!

Time of Reflections

____

____

____

____

____

June 16

Moving Forward, Manifesting Marvelous, Monday! You will Never be The Same Again. I receive and accept that this morning. Is just been in my spirit for the past two days. So I just say yes Lord. It is well with my soul. God thank you for allowing me to rest in you last night. I just sleep in the arms of MY EVERYTHING! God bless you all this day. Be encouraged and keep looking up and holding on! Things will get better after while.

Time of Reflections

____

____

____

____

____

June 17

There is no other way to start this day off without giving God the glory due to Him on this Thanking God, Trusting in him, Turning it Around Tuesday! I pray this will be a bless week for all my family, friends, love ones, COGFBJC, BABM, HUSTY, and the list goes on until it includes you somewhere in the list. May the blessings of God allow this to be one of the best weeks of 2014. Yes, we are in the 6th month of the year. And in two weeks this month will be gone. We must make sure we live, love and laugh. Just be happy in Jesus no matter what come or go just count it all joy. The joy of the Lord is my strength and they that wait upon the Lord shall renew their strength. God has you covered and just keep on looking up and depending on Him. After it is all said and done where you start out with Him, or in the middle of you situation, or at the end; you have no choice but to go to Him. He will not hold this against you. So seek ye first the Kingdom of God and all these other things will be added unto you!

Time of Reflections

____

____

____

____

____

June 18

Walk with me Lord, Working, Wonderful, Worshipping him Wednesday! It's another day the Lord has kept me. Yes, it is 11:59 so 12:00 makes it a new day for all of us rather you are awake or sleep. God and his angels are watching over us all. I hope and trust that this day finds you in the best of health, and strength that life has to offer us all. Remember there is a Balm in Gilead to heal the sin sick souls. Do not worry about what this day is going to bring you, but see what you can add to this day to make it better for yourself and someone else. God is really good. I don't have all the sleep I need right now but I know somebody is praying for me. There will be a testimony after this that God brought me over. I look at now and I yet thank Him for what lies ahead and then once I reach my Harvestville Destination, then I can say, How I got over, How I got over my soul looks back and wonder how I got over! God is great and greatly to be praised. Enjoy your day and let someone else know that God is worthy to be praised.

Time of Reflections

____

____

____

____

____

June 19

He is preparing me for my greater and through the eyes of faith my greater is around the corner. I encourage you that your greater is on the way. That what you have been praying and believing God for, it's almost at your front door. God might didn't send it Federal Express but he wanted you to trust and rely on him. So He has already worked it out for you on this Triumphant, Turning it Around Thursday! Just be both happy and encouraged because He has already worked it out for you. You are in your due season. So be not weary in well doing for in due season, you will reap and faint not. So, the seeds that you have sown are coming up in your harvest season. Have a great day and just give Him glory and praise on this day and every day.

Time of Reflections

____

____

____

____

____

June 20

Faithful to believe Friday! Jesus, Jesus, sweet Jesus, Jesus oh how I love to call on your name. Sometimes in the morning, sometimes late at night when I call on your name Jesus everything was alright . . . . There is something about the name of Jesus. When you call the name of Jesus prayer changes things. I yet give God a Right Now Praise for A Right Now Change. I will hold fast to this. It's been over a month He gave me that slogan. I refuse to believe anything different. I just bless His name. I encourage you today that He is moving all up in your situation. YOU cannot see what changes are being made because you are stuck on the past but once you release the past then you can take a peek into your future and know God is yet working it out for you. I feel like shouting GLORY this morning. If you feel your prayers are not being answered, then change the way you pray. If you don't know what to say, just say Lord teach me how to pray and what to say. Then He will make intercession on your behalf. God is just good. I want take nothing for my journey right now. When God begin to move and answering your prayers it's going to be happening so quick until you want believe it's happening to and for you. REMAIN faithful, dedicated and committed to HIM. He is able, capable and willing to handle everything for you. Have a triumphant Thursday and whatever you do this day; just put it ALL in His Hands! It makes all the difference. Rejoice and be glad and again I say REJOICE . . . .

Time of Reflections

____

____

____

____

____

June 21

Yes, Yes, Yes, it is now Shaping Up, Standing Still Saturday! I hope and trust it will be such a day for you. When you have worked all week, you want the last day of the work week to close with a good bang. Whatever happened this week, leave it in the past nothing you can change so leave it and move forward on this weekend. There's no need of worrying about what tomorrow is going to bring; it will be all over in the morning. In the morning, morning, it will be all over in the morning. Wow, that song blessed my soul and it is morning so what you went through yesterday or last night IT'S OVER. Lord, continue to do great and mighty things for my family, friends, church members, Husty, BABM, and the Church of God Founded By Jesus Christ, Inc. There are things that man can do, He can sail through the air in his plane but no man can do a lot of things, man he's limited. Tell me can you catch the wind, can you make the world spin, can you pull the sun down, can you make man from the ground, OH NO, BUT I KNOW WHO CAN, GOD CAN! With that in mind know God can do all things. So this too it only came to pass. Keep the faith and watch God turn it around for YOU . . . . My Friends have a wonderful and Super Day!

Time of Reflections

____

____

____

____

____

June 22

Its Super Sunny Serving the Lord with gladness Sunday! I am so grateful to see this day. I give God all the praise and glory for the things that he has done. If it wasn't for him where would we be. God is just good like that! All I can say is Thank You Jesus! You are the best Thing That Ever Happened To Me. I hope and trust that as we go through this day let us think about the goodness of Jesus and all that He has done for us. When praises go up the blessings come down. WE don't praise Him to receive anything but we give Him praise because of who He is. Wonderful, counselor, mighty God, Prince of Peace and the list goes on and on. Who is He to you this Day? I will start the answer session He Is My All and All "MY EVERYTHING" BABM . . . . Enjoy your wonderful day and let go and Let God in your life on This Spirit Touch Me One More Time Sunday!

Time of Reflections

June 23

Without you, without you, I can't win this fight without you! I am not worried about tomorrow I just live from day to day . . . . Don't know all of it but the joy bells just flood my soul this Moving Forward, Manifesting Monday morning. I just thank God for his love. Until I just have to embrace Him back. He is so good to us all. Was there ever a time in your life that you called on Jesus and He didn't show up. As John Pee Kee says, He will show up on Time. Just know when you feel like things are falling apart, know it's for a reason because after that, the potter will put you back together again. Once He put things and you back together again, then you can truly say, THERE WILL BE JOY AFTER THIS! THERE WILL BE A TESTIMONY AFTER THIS! So sit back and count it all joy because your Joy and Testimony is coming through. Then you can say, "I know it was Jesus that did this" and He shall receive the glory. Let us go and give God the praise that is really due to him. Let us give him a new and different praise on this day I still believe that A Right Now Praise is going to Give Us That Right Now Change . . . . It want always be like this, He's Turning It Around for You! I love each of you and God bless you this day and everyday . . . .

Time of Reflections

____

____

____

____

____

June 24

Talk To Jesus, Telling of his goodness Tuesday! Lord, this morning I don't want to talk to man but I want to talk to the individual spirit of man that will reach their soul on this morning. God only you can touch the inner heart of man. As we jump start this day just let your glory and peace rest upon each individual that is going to read this. I need you to really show up and minister to the spirit man. You be the leader, the guide, and help us to stay focus on you no matter what. You have done too and so much and looking back is not an option. The only time I feel we should look back is to see how far God brought us from. There are some individuals (souls) that have been assigned to my hands. I am praying and not going to give up and one reason God didn't give up on us, therefore we cannot give up on people. God just keep them in the ark of safety this day and do something really special. You know the heart and you know the plan and purpose in which you have set out for our lives. God I want you to rule and super rule in every individual life that is going to read this, I want you to shake, stir, and seal some things up for them. I trust you and know that you are not slack concerning your promises but you would fulfill that what you said that you would do. When things get rough and tough, we may feel like the easy thing to do is give up and throw in the towel but my brothers and sisters we cannot afford to do so. WE must endure hardness as a good soldier. So with that in mind we must MOVE FORWARD and allow God to take full control of our lives. WE must surrender and give Him all of us. Once we give Him all of us, we can see that the strong holds are being broken and the chains been broken as well. God has an assignment with your name on it. You may sway here and there but before it is all said and done you have to ask yourself WILL MY SPIRIT SAY YES? WE must say yes Lord, yes to your will and yes to your way. God is yet on the throne and all we have to do is have a little talk with him and tell him about out troubles he will hear our cry and He will answer by and by so go to him and GET YOUR ANSWER FROM GOD on what direction you need to go and what you need to do. LET GO AND LET GOD! I STILL HAVE A RIGHT NOW PRAISE FOR A RIGHT NOW CHANGE! BABM, HUSTY, TP &D, Mt Zion, Church of God Founded BY Jesus Christ, family Friends and Love Ones we might as well praise Him in Advance.... I will start it off by just shouting GLORY TO HIS NAME, GO Into your Worship Zone....

Time of Reflections

____

____

____

____

____

June 25

Walking With Him, Worshipping With God, Waiting on Jesus Wednesday! God is so awesome and amazing. He is the great I am. Know that the Lord has seen your tears and has heard your prayers so HE has taken action on your behalf. Yes, God is blessing you right now oh right now, He woke you up this morning and started you on your way, the Lord is blessing you right now. WE just have to learn to put it on the ALTAR. He will work it out for you, you and especially you. I am happy in Jesus. If you only knew what the Lord has in store for you, you would be clapping your hands, you would be dancing, and leaping for joy if you only knew. And if you don't know, you can still offer up Him some praises as well. Your praise will move GOD and allow Him to Take Action on Your Behalf. BABM with that said and done, I am now released to change my signature. I was praying and seeking God that I wasn't going to change it. But ARNC has been build, and in a home to do what needs to be done so I give Him glory for allowing the saying to come alive and manifest itself to us all! Don't stop praising Him . . . .

Time of Reflections

June 26

God is a good God, Yes He Is, Yes He Is, Yes He Is. If you haven't tried him lately, then I encourage you to take the time to do so. His name is wonderful Jesus Christ our Lord. He woke me up early this morning feeling good and giving Him praises. Yes, it is another Triumphant, Turning it Around, Trying Jesus Thursday! I was made and commanded to praise God. This is my purpose and to obey His commandments. There is a blessing in doing so. I wouldn't take anything for my journey right now. People of God be Determined to hold on a little while longer as God reveal His plan for your life. The Best is Yet to Come and through the eyes of FAITH, the Best is already here. Keep Holding On to God's Unchanging Hands. He want let it go. God bless you this day and the things you have been praying about that it will manifest This Day!! Keep Moving Forward. I love you all.

Time of Reflections

____

____

____

____

____

June 27

Fix It Jesus, Faith, From Defeat to Victory Friday! I cannot seem to thank Him enough. I can never repay you Lord for what you done for me, how you lose the shuckles and set me free, how you made a way out of no way turned my darkness into day . . . . Lord, you been so faithful. God is so great and we must give Him the glory and praise. This is the day the Lord has made we will rejoice and be glad in it. So let us give God a high praise on this Fruitful Finally Friday is here! Just be encouraged because this week is just about over. WE made it this far and God is going to allow us to make it a little further. God bless you all!

Time of Reflections

____

____

____

____

____

June 28

This may be your prayer and desire on this Still got a praise on the inside Super, Saturday! Clean this house from the inside out. Lord, restore me from the inside out. God is a God of restoration. He will fix whatever is broken in your life and he will restore you. For Jeremiah said it like this, Go down to the potters house and let the potter put you back together again. You who are broken inside, allow God to mend you this day. God is a heart fixer and a mind regulator. We must press like Apostle Paul said. I feel like pressing my way, I feel like pressing my way, though trails come on every hand; I feel like pressing my way. So you have to have a determined mind that you are going to press no matter what. It may seems hard and difficult right now and you are at the crossroad of life wondering which way to turn. But just listen to the voice of God, He will lead and direct you in the path that you should go. The question becomes are you willing to follow the plan that God has destined for your life? He knows the plan that you take. So let him guide your steps and allow him to lead you this day. As I close this thought on this Super Standing Still Saturday, the songs says Follow Jesus, take no chance at getting lost, Follow Jesus, He has a plan to take you to the top and if He doesn't then there is no one who can . . . . Who will you follow this day? I am glad I have decided to follow Jesus, I have decided to follow Jesus, No turning back, oh no, no turning back. The cross before me, the world behind me, the cross before me, the world behind me, no turning back, oh no, no turning back!

Time of Reflections

____

____

____

____

____

June 29

The last Standing Still, Showing the Love of Jesus, Stirring Up down in my Soul Sunday! Every time I turn around the Lord is blessing me, Every time I turn around the Lord is keeping me, so I just say Glory, thank you Lord, He is blessing me. Seem like it was very difficult to post this one this morning but I always get the victory in the end. Yes, what a good way to jumpstart this Super Sunday knowing that you are blessed. Sometimes we take things for granted but we must look around at other people sometimes to realize how bless we really have it. There are people who do not have life, health, nor strength to do what they want to do without waiting on someone else to get it done for them. We can get up and do what we want to do and when we want to do it. This is a blessing not having to wait around on people to get things done. Let us just take this day to reflect on those who do not have all their limbs and the use of their limbs. They would love to have the same opportunity that we have to be able to do some things they haven't done in a while. Things people would appreciate to do or have, while we that have and can do take it for granted. It is just by God's grace and mercy that things are well as they are with us because it could be the other way. Let us be more thankful today than we were on yesterday. Imagine a day without your legs, eyes, hearing, hands .... How would life be for you? Now give God praise that you are able to walk, talk, see, hear, smell and do for yourself. God bless you this day as we remember those who are unable to do the things we do. Whisper a prayer that God will bless and keep them forever in His care.

Time of Reflections

____

____

____

____

____

June 30

Made Up My Mind, Moving Forward Monday! Before I got in the shower this song came to my mind to encourage someone this morning WHERE EVER YOU ARE AND WHATEVER YOU GOING THROUGH, GOD SAID THE STRUGGLE IS OVER FOR YOU . . . . LET IT BLESS YOUR SOUL and apply it to your life PERSONALLY . . . . GOD SAID THE STRUGGLE IS OVER FOR YOU!

I am rejoicing in the God of my salvation. There is no hurt that he cannot heal all things work according to the master's perfect will so this battle is not yours it's the Lord. Yes, whatever you faced with this past week, today starts a brand new week and a new chapter in your life. Since you are here at this point you might as well . . . . Rejoice and Give Him Praise, Glory and The Honor. You thought you had to fight in this battle but little that you know GOD already won the battle for you. He just wanted us to show up and be in position to allow the enemy to know we are not scared to show up, because God is going to show out and handle this battle. Lord, I feel like preaching but it's not my time. If you got a problem in your life or battle take it to Jesus, seem like nothing ever turn out right take it to Jesus, take it to Jesus, see I tried him for myself and I don't need no one else Jesus will make Everything Alright . . . . Want He Do It? Yes, He Will. My God, My God. I am so caught up today. I got to get through this day. I would hold my mew but if I do that then the rocks will cry out! This is not so on my clock.

Time of Reflections

___

___

___

___

___

Month Seven

July

July 1

Thanking God for this Terrific, Taking it to Jesus Tuesday! Everyone be safe today. It is raining hard. I look at it like this God is showering his blessings down on us. Allow God to arise in your life and the enemies be scattered so send the praise up to God on this thanking him Tuesday and watch the unexpected blessings come down. Any praisers around? Who is willing to praise him inspite of your situation on this day? Rejoice He is turning it around for you!

Time of Reflections

July 2

I give you the glory, I give you the honor, I give you the praise forever and ever, I will lift up your name . . . . I give you the glory, I give you the honor, I give you the praise forever and ever, I will lift up your name . . . .

Thanking God for another wonderful worshipping Wednesday that lies ahead for all of us. In all things we have to give thanks. God we need you now, we need you now, we need you now, we need you now. Not another second, or another minute, not another hour or another day with our arms out stretched we need you right away . . . . I will hold on and hold out until my change come. Sometimes things get a little rocky and shaky for us all but we have to know in whom we believe in and who's we are. We have to have that determined faith as the Hebrew boys had, if God don't do it, I know that He is able to deliver us this day! God is a deliverer. I say hold on my brother and sister your change is going to come, be strong for your work is not done, He is able to give you joy in the morning light . . . . I decree and declare it right now. I take authority that God has given me, and I make this request known unto Him this day. When you praise the Lord, He will fight your battle for the battle belongs to the Lord. WE are going to put down the carnal weapons and pick up the weapons of praise for the Battle Belongs to the Lord. I just experienced a hangover from this past Sunday, There is No Need TO Fight . . . . So just bless His name because you showed up to it. That was your only purpose was to show up. That lets the enemy know, he doesn't scare you. Enjoy your terrific telling the devil it just won't work Wednesday. Whatever comes this day or comes up DIJWW (Devil It Just Won't Work). Be forever blessed and inspired through His Word. We are working for Jesus and we have to go through.

Time of Reflections

____

____

____

____

____

July 3

Through thick and thin, trampling over the enemy Thursday! Today is the day the Lord has made, l will rejoice and be glad in it! I give you all of me. Yes, my worship is for real. It's another day's journey and l am glad about it. God is calling us to our greater and it removes us out of our comfort zone into a place of doing his will. God use us for your glory! All of this came in order to pass. You have one more river to cross and God will get you to the other side of your through. Be forever Bless!

Time of Reflections

____

____

____

____

____

July 4

Happy 4th of July to everyone. I pray this Fret Not, Forgiven, Faithful to believe Friday will bring Sunshine your way on this lovely day. Know that God is still in charge of your life. When we give it to Him, he will work it out for us. My brothers and sisters just look up knowing that your Redeemer draweth nigh. There is a praise on the inside that I can't keep to myself Holla stirring up down in my soul . . . . So excuse me if I seem a little strange but praise is the way I say thank YOU! What better way to thank God and give him the praise for what He has done in your life, for you this day, and what He is even going to do. Continue to allow God to bless you in deed. There is a storm out on the ocean and it is moving this oh way and if your souls is not anchored in Jesus you will surely drift away. Be very sure that your anchor hold and grip that solid Rock. Yes, it is Jesus. I love you all and God bless you continually . . . .

Time of Reflections

____

____

____

____

____

July 5

Greetings hope everyone had a great day yesterday! Today is a new day and the song that really blessed me at 5 am was Thank You Lord For all You Done For Me. What a way to begin this Shaking the Devil off, somebody had me on their mind Saturday! This take cares all aspects of life and l really say Thank You Lord for all You Done For Me! It could've been me but thanks be to, GOD for His mercy, grace and FAVOR! God is up to something great be encouraged because it may not look or seem like it but God has taken action on your behalf. My brothers and sisters keep on praying for the LORD is Nigh, keep on praying; he will hear our cry for the LORD has PROMISED and His Word is True don't stop praying He'll answer You!

Time of Reflections

____

____

____

____

____

July 6

He brought me through this, He brought me through that yes l am grateful to you! Giving God praise on this Still holding On, Stepping on Sunday! I hope and trust that this would be a lovely day for each of you. May you get accomplish that what you need to on this day. Don't forget to give God some praise on today. As good as God been to me l can't afford not to praise his Name. So just praise Him because of who He is. He Is My Everything. BABM l played it in the midnight hour and just loved and squeezed on it. Lord l just want to thank you and yes He is still working on me. I am not yet where l want to be but l am on the freeway that is going to take me to the plan God wants me to fulfill in my life. Sorry to take your name but the way l am feeling this day l am Destined for Purpose as well! I can't explain it but God Knows!

Time of Reflections

____

____

____

____

____

July 7

Make me over again wash me in your blood, wash me over again. Yes, it is another Lord's day and I am glad about it. We are not exempt from trials or tribulations but we must be conditioned to go through. The song writer wrote, I am conditioned to go through, I don't mind, I don't mind, I don't mind. We shall come out as pure gold. I will say it like this, the hotter the fire the shiner you would come out. After it is all said and done, we don't look like what we been through. As you go to the Lord house just praise God as never before. Your breakthrough is in your praise. I refuse to lose my praise. Have yourself a Making Me Happy and Making Me Whole Moving Forward Monday! When we smile, we let God know through faith that I Believe It Is Going To Be Alright. Much love and peace for each of you this day!

Time of Reflections

____

____

____

____

____

July 8

Lord prepare me to be a sanctuary, tried and true, and with thanksgiving I'll be a living sanctuary Lord for you. What a way to start a new week with a melody ringing down inside of our heart. We say God is awesome but do we really know just how awesome He really is. I want to know him more and more in the power of his resurrection. He is all mighty and powerful, there is nothing he want to for his children if we delight ourselves in him. If we do that, then he will give us the desires of our heart! Be blessed on this take me back, trusting him Tuesday!

Time of Reflections

____

____

____

____

____

July 9

Yes, take me to the king this telling of His goodness Wednesday! Work it out, Well Please Wednesday if you would Lord Jesus. If it had not been for the Lord on our side then where would we be. He told us, He will never leave us nor forsake us and He will be with us even to the end of the world. That is worth shouting Glory for. You just don't know just how good God been to me. Through storms and rain l made it. What about you? Just enjoy and love on him today as you share His goodness. Yes, you ain't seen nothing yet. There is another blessing with your name on it. So are you going to praise Him in advance or what. Hold it a second l know l am. God Bless each of you!

Time of Reflections

____

____

____

____

____

July 10

Oh Lord How Excellent Is Thy Name In All The Earth? There is none like you. On this Through thick and thin, Trampling over the enemy Thursday! We have to realize nothing is going to happen today that God and I cannot handle. We are at the halfway point in the week and God is able to do a drastic change in your situation. As an act of faith just turn around three times and tell God that you thank Him for turning it around for you. The people of God go through so much but it's only to help us get to the plan and will of God. We have no choice but to surrender if we want to make it to heaven. Stop fighting and struggling with the same thing day in and day out. God has left some things in our hands to do and until we do that CHANGE will not be manifested. We can't see the forest because of the trees in our view. Let this message minister to your spirit today! Its for me as well as for you.

Time of Reflections

____

____

____

____

____

July 11

Fret Not, Forgiven, Faithful to Believe Friday! Psalm 124:1-2,6-8. If it had not been the Lord who was on our side, now may Israel say; If it had not been the Lord who was on our side, when men rose up against us: Blessed be the Lord, who hath not given us as a prey to their teeth. Our soul is escaped as a bird out of the snare of the fowlers: the snare is broken, and we are escaped. Our help is in the name of the Lord, who made heaven and earth.

Time of Reflections

____

____

____

____

____

July 12

Shaking the Devil off, Somebody had me on their Mind Saturday! God is yet in the blessing business. We must continue to seek the face of the Lord. We must keep our hands in his hands and move forward no matter what come or go. We must keep the faith in him, don't put your trust and confidence in man for they will let you down. TP & Deliverance is celebrating its 11th Rainbow Tea. Don't miss this event today at 6:00pm.

Time of Reflections

____

____

____

____

____

July 13

This is the day the Lord has made, l will rejoice and be glad it is! I am excited about what this day is going to bring. There is a super gladness going on in the inside on this Still Holding On, Stepping On Sunday! This joy l have the world didn't give it to me and l refuse to let the world take it away. My motivational thought to each of us today is to keep on keeping on and keep on holding on. It's going to pay off after awhile. Have a super through the eyes of faith sunny Sunday!

Time of Reflections

July 14

Making Me Happy and Making Me whole Moving Forward Monday! Psalm 125:1. Thy that trust in the Lord shall be as mount Zion, which cannot be removed, but abideth for ever.

Time of Reflections

July 15

Yes, another Take me back, Trusting in him Tuesday! It is good to be on the Lord side. God is great and greatly to be praised. Thank God for the rest but He still got me up. Lord l am available to you. Use me Lord to show someone the way and if you can use anything Lord you can use me. Here am l Lord, speak and your servant heareth. This day allow God to speak to you. Hear His voice and do what He tells you to do! Be bless this day . . .

Time of Reflections

____

____

____

____

____

July 16

Work it Out, Well Please Wednesday! Psalms 125:4-5. Do good, O Lord, unto those that be good, and to them that are upright in their hearts. As for such as turn aside unto their crooked ways, the Lord shall lead them forth with the workers of iniquity: but peace shall be upon Israel.

Time of Reflections

____

____

____

____

____

July 17

Through thick and thin, Trampling over the enemy Thursday! As l prayed what to post on this wonderful working worshipping God Wednesday, here it is: I don't feel noways tired l come too far from where l started from nobody told me the road would be easy l don't believe he brought me this far to leave me. Know that every day may not go like you expect it to but know we will have some good days and some challenging days but the good days out weighs those not . . . so good days. With God we will get through every moment because he has provided a way for us to escape. In all things give thanks because every trail, for every mountain you see me through l lift my hands in total praise to you. I feel good this day every time l think about Jesus makes me feel good. Think about where God brought you from and bless his name while the glory of the Lord rise among you this day and everyday. I am yet saying Lord, Help Me. If you need his help ask him this day and l am convenience He will help you. There is no way l can live without YOU . . . .

Time of Reflections

July 18

Fret Not, Forgiven, Faithful to believe Friday! Psalm 126:3,5. The Lord hath done great things for us; whereof we are glad. They that sow in tears shall reap in joy.

Time of Reflections

July 19

Shaking the devil off, Somebody had me on their Mind Saturday! Psalm 127:1. Except the Lord build the house, they labour in vain that build it: except the Lord keep the city, the watchman waketh but in vain.

Time of Reflections

____

____

____

____

____

July 20

Still holding On, Stepping on Sunday! Psalm 128:1 blessed is everyone that feareth the Lord; that walketh in his ways.

Time of Reflections

____

____

____

____

____

July 21

Making Me Happy and Making Me Whole Moving Forward Monday! Psalm 128:2. For thou shalt eat the labour of thine hands: happy shalt thou be, and it shall be well with thee.

Time of Reflections

July 22

Take Me Back, Trusting in him Tuesday! Psalm 129:2,4. Many a time have they afflicted me from my youth: yet they have not prevailed against me. The Lord is righteous: he hath cut asunder the cords of the wicked.

Time of Reflections

July 23

Work it out, Well Please Wednesday! Psalm 130:1-2. Out of the depths have I cried unto thee, O Lord. Lord, hear my voice: let thine ears be attentive to the voice of my supplications.

Time of Reflections

____

____

____

____

____

July 24

Through thick and thin Trampling over the enemy Thursday! Victory is yours and mine this day. We have to tell satan just as Jesus told him, satan get thee behind. Then we move forward. Devil whatever you trying to do to attack the people of God, l bind you and all your attacks through the blood of Jesus, sickness, poverty, stress, depression, negative thoughts, sadness, loneness and all others that l cannot call at this time be though remove right name and . . . we declare and decree health, wealth, peace, prosperity, determination, faith, joy, gentleness to enter in this day as we stay focus and acknowledge God in all our ways so he can direct our paths. Let Jesus lead you, you and especially you this day. Whatever is holding you or got you bound release it right now. I am a firm believer that when God blesses you he add no sorrow with it! Just worship Him this day. Your victory and breakthrough is in your praise. God Bless Each Of You!

Time of Reflections

____

____

____

____

____

July 25

Fret Not, Forgiven, Faithful to Believe Friday! Psalm 130:5-6. I wait for the Lord, my soul doth wait, and in his word do I hope. My soul waiteth for the Lord more than they that watch for the morning: I say, more than they that watch for the morning.

Time of Reflections

____

____

____

____

____

July 26

Shaking the devil Off, Somebody had me on their Mind Saturday! Psalm 132:12. If thy children will keep my covenant and my testimony that I shall teach them, their children shall also sit upon thy throne for evermore.

Time of Reflections

____

____

____

____

____

July 27

Still holding on, Stepping On Sunday! Jesus rested on the seventh day, why can't we. Just a fruitful thought but we have to keep moving forward. One thing for sure God will always help us out in all our doings. For you that is wondering when your turn around is coming, it's not long l say to you this day, hang on in there, hold on your change is coming sooner than you think. You are going to make it so don't worry about a thing. In times like this trust God the more and release your faith the more. Don't give up on God because He never gave up on us despite our shortcomings He still loved us. When we don't see things happening as soon as we should at times that doesn't mean God is not working on your behalf. If He done it before, He will do it again! Praise God this day from whom all blessings flow and there are some headed your way. God is not through blessing you!

Time of Reflections

____

____

____

____

____

July 28

Making Me Happy and Making Me Whole Moving Forward Monday! Psalm 133:1. Behold, how good and how pleasant it is for brethren to dwell together in unity.

Time of Reflections

____

____

____

____

____

July 29

Trusting in Jesus, Thanking God Tuesday! Psalm 134:1-2. Behold, Bless ye thee Lord, all ye servants of the Lord, which by night stand in the house of the Lord. Lift up your hands in the sanctuary, and bless the Lord.

Time of Reflections

____

____

____

____

____

July 30

Work it out, Well Please Wednesday! Psalm 135:1-3. Praise Ye the Lord. Praise ye the name of the Lord; praise him, O ye servants of the Lord. Ye that stand in the house of the Lord, in the courts of the house of our God, Praise the Lord; for the Lord is good: sing praises unto his name; for it is pleasant.

Time of Reflections

____

____

____

____

____

July 31

This is the day God has made I am going to rejoice and be glad in it. Through thick and thin Trampling over the enemy Thursday we are going to make it. God has given us power over satan. We can defeat him and he knows he is a defeated foe. God has already won the battle for us. We have to keep praising God and giving him the glory for all that he is doing and going to do for each one of us. Count it all joy inspite of what it looks like right now. There are better days ahead for us.

Time of Reflections

Month Eight

August

August 1

Faithful to believe Following him Friday! My Greater is closer than it appears! I just give him Glory on this day! I yet make it known to satan and all of his amps; Devil it Just Want Work. DJWW. God has a plan and it would be fulfilled. I am pressing on the upper way new heights I am gaining each and every day. Lord lift me up and let me stand, place my feet on solid ground. I shall not be MOVED nor BROKEN! Get thee hence satan and all that allows him to use them . . . .

Time of Reflections

____

____

____

____

____

August 2

Super, Standing Still, Shaping up Saturday! All that I am and all that l hope to be, I'm fully committed to your will and to your way. I'll make the sacrifice to do what you asked of me, yes, yeah, heah! For the rest of my life I'm sold out, I'm going to hold out. So on this fantastic faithful to believe Fully Committed Friday, just allow God to be your Everything. Know this one thing that God is still in control. If we only acknowledge Him, then he will direct us in the direction we suppose to take. Sometimes we get so caught up with the world and the issues in our life until we don't pause and say Lord, Help Me. As you become more committed for His use and service ask God to help you this day and I am firm believer that he will do it. I decree and declare whoever reads this on today, Lord that you will help them and meet every individual need this day as they commit themselves to you totally, in Jesus name. Amen!

Time of Reflections

____

____

____

____

____

August 3

Super Shouting, Spirit Fall Down on Me Sunday! Psalm 135:13. Thy name, O Lord, endureth for ever; and thy memorial, O Lord, throughout all generations.

Time of Reflections

____

____

____

____

____

August 4

Made up My Mind, Moving Forward Monday! I am walking in authority for the victory has been won concerning you. It may seem that you are losing, has lost, but I want you to know God has won the victory for you in your situation. Your name is Victory. God was not going to let you go out like that without you coming out victoriously. Whatever you want God to do for you and bring you out of l decree and declare that God has moved and worked it out for you. The time is now to release and let go of the past and move forward. Better days are ahead just for you. It's only a test you had to go through but l can hear the spirit of the Lord saying your test and struggle is over in this particular season. My God, My God . . . . l feel my two step dance coming on right about now. Lord l hear you, l trust and believe you! We bind up confusion, depression, stress and sickness and we lose healing this day in the name of Jesus. Lord Do It For Us Right Now! Have a Marvelous Monday. God bless each of you.

Time of Reflections

____

____

____

____

____

August 5

Trusting in Him, Turing it Around Tuesday! Psalm 137:4,9. How shall we sing the Lord's song in a strange land? Happy shall he be, that taketh and dasheth thy little ones against the stones.

Time of Reflections

August 6

Waiting On Jesus, Worshipping Walking in Divine Purpose Wednesday! Psalm 138:1. I will praise thee with my whole heart: before the gods will I sing praise unto thee. In the day when I cried thou answeredst me, and strengthenedst me with strength in my soul.

Time of Reflections

August 7

Triumphant, taking it to Jesus Thursday! Psalm 139:7-8. Though I walk in the midst of trouble, thou wilt revive me: thou shalt stretch forth thine hand against the wrath of mine enemies, and thy right hand shall save me. The Lord will perfect that which concerneth me: thy mercy, O Lord, endureth for ever: forsake not the works of thine own hands.

Time of Reflections

____

____

____

____

____

August 8

Fret not, Forgiven, Faithful to believe Friday! Why should l feel discourage and why should my heart feel lonely and long for my heaven at home, when Jesus is my fortress a constant friend is he, his eyes are on the sparrow and l know he watches me. God we trust you this day move mightily and as never before. Help us this day in the name of Jesus. We must look to the hills from whence cometh our help ALL our help comes from the Lord. Have a bless and enjoyable day. He's Got You this day and every day, also in every situation.

Time of Reflections

____

____

____

____

____

August 9

Shaping Up, Shaking It Off, Super Standing Still Saturday! Psalm 139:1-2. O Lord, thou hast searched me, and known me. Thou knowest my downsitting and mine uprising, thou understandest my thought afar off.

Time of Reflections

____

____

____

____

____

August 10

Still Holding On, Stepping On the Upward Way Sunday! Psalm 139:7. Whither shall I go from thy spirit? Or whither shall I flee from thy presence? Stay in the presence of the Lord. Where the spirit of the Lord is there is liberty! You can be free as long as you stay in his presence.

Time of Reflections

____

____

____

____

____

August 11

Making Me Happy and Making Me Whole Moving Forward Monday! Psalm139:8-10. If I ascend up into heaven, thou art there: if I make my bed in hell, behold, thou art there. If I take the wings of the morning, and dwell in the uttermost parts of the sea; Even there shall thy hand lead me, and thy right hand shall hold me.

Time of Reflections

____

____

____

____

____

August 12

Trusting Him, Taking it to Jesus, Tried by the Fire Tuesday! Allow your faith to convenience you that God is your Everything! I know he is My Everything. What is He to you this day? Don't let nothing shake your faith in God. He is the only one we have to rely and trust in.

Time of Reflections

____

____

____

____

____

August 13

Wonderful Worshipping Walking in His Divine Purpose Wednesday! Lord l just want to thank you for the storm on last night cause it helped me to sleep that much harder. I give God praise for allowing me to see what l decree and declare a worship experience like no other as throw things behind me and Walk Forward in your purpose for my life. Leave the past in the past and everyday is a new day so we must treat it as such. God is an awesome God. I ask myself where would I be without Him. I know l never would have made it this far without Him. I have been praying for each of you now l need each of you to stand in the gap for me. Pray today and ask God to move on my behalf. We all need prayer and when people ask for prayer we take for so l can continue to stand and move forward to my purpose. I thank you in advance because I know the prayers of the righteous availeth much! Enjoy your terrific telling of His goodness Tuesday. I challenge each of us to tell three people about his goodness via text, phone, e-mail or in person and Watch what God does for you.

Time of Reflections

August 14

There will be Mountains as we trust in the Lord with all our heart Thursday! Welcome into this place, welcome into this broken vessel you desire to abide in the presences of your people so we lift our hands and we lift our hearts as we offer up this praise unto your name. What a way to start this day off as the praise just go forth down in our soul. God is able to see us through any situation. There is nothing too hard for our God. We have to continue to put our trust in Jesus and He will make everything alright. Let us continue to pray for the family of those deceased. Pray that God will strengthen the hearts and fill the void that has been taken away. God; we need your help today, tomorrow and all the days that lies ahead. God only you can get us through the darkest hour of the night. Hold us and rock us in your arms. Thank you in advance for doing it for the families, friends and our love ones. Amen! Do the best you can this day. God is looking down on us.

Time of Reflections

August 15

Forsake All Others, Following Jesus all the Way, Faithful to believe Friday! What a mighty God we serve! I was able to sleep real well. Thank you Jesus I feel a difference. Don't know what this day is going to bring, but l pray it would be a bless day for us all. God is yet in the blessing business. When praises go up blessings come down. Yet thanking God there's no pain in this body at all. We don't know how bless we really are until we just look around and think things over, then we can truly say that we are bless. So if you don't know it let me share with you that you are bless. Success shouldn't be based on what you have materialistic but what you have prepared for eternal in to heaven. I decree and declare this day, our Greater is Coming! Keep expecting because it is on the way.

Time of Reflections

____

____

____

____

____

August 16

So Glad I am Here Super, Standing Still Saturday! He is good. Just to encourage you this day, but they that wait upon the Lord, shall renew their strength, they shall mount up like wings as Eagles; they shall run, and not be weary; they shall walk, and not faint. So God is allowing you to soar on this day. Just know that He loves you and He cares for you! Since it is Saturday it doesn't take much motivation to get us through this day knowing that we are doing what we need to get done or want to do! God bless each of you this day as He does every day!

Time of Reflections

____

____

____

____

____

August 17

I love the Lord on this Super, Shouting, Standing on a Sure Foundation Sunday! God is yet in the blessing business. Often times we say he may not come when you want him but he is always on time. I say bless his name for showing up because even if we think he doesn't show up, He always works it out for us. This is the last free weekend and then work bound for another exciting, super, cool school year. It is well with my soul. Let us start praying in advance for the schools as a whole, administrators, teachers, support staff, custodians, cafeteria workers, bus drivers, students, parents, guardian/caregivers. Hope no one is left out and if so that means for you too. Congratulations to each of you as you receive your greater. I rejoice with you because it is yet on the way!

Time of Reflections

___

___

___

___

___

August 18

Moving Forward, Making things Happen for you Monday! What a mighty good time we had today at Total Praise & Deliverance the word for today was "STEP BACK AND LET GOD DO IT" The Battle is not yours but its the Lords. God moved in a mighty way. God is not short concerning His promises but he will do that what He said he will do. God bless each of you all and have a nice night and allow the Word to meditate within your spirit and in your soul. GOD IS THE ONE THAT CAN HANDLE ANY SITUATION. A lot of times I mention and talk about coming out and praising God because mine is based on praising God and teaching people how to become delivered. Pray for me and I will continue to pray for you!

The enemy don't won't me to post this morning but h is defeated. I pray this day that God will see each of us through this day. We must be lead by him and walk in Hs Divine Purpose for our life. Saints of the living God it is high time now to hold on and grab hold to that Holy Grip of Jesus Christ Himself. Don't let go and don't give up. Suppose God would have given up on us. Don't give up on God . . . because He won't give up on us, He is able. If you only knew that you were at your breakthrough point, you will keep on keeping on. Its not as long as it was but since you can see the sun praise the rest of your way out of this and that. Its over now, you can and will make it. Now, you can say, How l got over, How l got over my soul looks back and wonder how l got over. Believe God this day for every spoken word in your life. It is So and It is Done because it has been decreed and declared in Jesus's Name. Amen!

Time of Reflections

____

____

____

____

____

August 19

Thanking God for another Marvelous Returning Back to Work Monday! God bless all of us this day and everyday to come. God has His hands on you! When God has His hands on you we are different individuals for the Bible says that we are a peculiar people. So let people try to figure us out and while they are doing that, God is moving us on to something else and doing more great things in our lives . . . . You do not know who I am unless you get to know the God within me. Even with that you will never know all about me. The more we want to get to know someone we should be the same way of really getting to know God. To know Him is to love Him cause God is love. Take the time this day and one on one just let Him know how much you really thank and appreciate Him for all that He's done for you. Words cannot express the zillion of things God has done for us. But I must say He's been good to me from my BIRTH up to this PRESENT TIME. Just in case He doesnt do anything else God knows He's done enough. Not only that, but I know if I continue in His Word, Obey and Do what it says do, then there is no good thing that He will withhold from me nor you! So Get what God has for you and Move Forward (BABM)! I love each of you.

Time of Reflections

____

____

____

____

____

August 20

I am chasing after you, no matter what l have to go through, just to be closer to you, cause l need you more and more. Yes its day two of this wonderful week. Thanking God for this tremendous, telling of his goodness, trusting more on Him Tuesday. Just a closer with thee is all l desire. We must move forward and presevere through the good and the bad. When you do not know what to do just stand sti . . . ll and ask God to help you. I promise you this day He will come to your rescue. Sometimes the human side may ask the two questions what's the point in it or what's the use. The answer goes way beyond this point of our earthly lives. Eternal life is what we are working for and trying to make it in the Kingdom of God. I got heaven in my view! I wanna go to heaven. Lord as l close this inspiration on today, l pray you will teach me your ways, and help me to understand the things l need to understand and that what l don't dismiss it from my mind. Allow me to Move Forward as l grow more in you. Help me this day and give me my daily bread and lead us not into temptation but deliver us from evil, for thine is the kingdom, the power and the glory, Amen! Thank you Jesus and l am going to love you forever.

Time of Reflections

August 21

Thanking God for another Wonderful Working Power Winning Worshipping Wednesday! I give you praise Lord for who you are in my life. Without you I can do nothing, without you, I would fail, without my whole life would be drifted without a sail. Thank you for all that you have done for me and continually to do for me and your children. David said it best in the book of Psalms, If it had not been . . . for the Lord on my side then where would we be today. Just take this time to thank God that he brought us from a mighty long ways and we definitely don't look like what we have been through. There are some hills we have to climb, there are some valleys we have to go through but in the mist of it all and every situation God is still God. He is our Giant Over Disasters on this day and every day. He is there for us all the time and when things get rough just say or whisper, Lord, Help Me! Without God, Without God we can't win this fight without Him; therefore, we have to Step Back and Let God Do It. Are you willing to Step Back This Day and Allow God to do it for you. My family, friends, and love ones he wants to do it for you, he is ready, he is willing, and he is able to do it for each of us. Just Say LORD DO IT FOR ME about three times and be sincere within your heart and by the end of the day the things that you ask Him to do, some of it will be done and worked out for you.

Time of Reflections

August 22

At 1:10 in the morning God is still good. Yes, in your late midnight hour God is turning it around for you! Know that somebody prayed for you in your midnight hour and your morning/dawning of a new day is approaching you. God bless you dearly.

Will someone help me lift him up on this Triumphant Thursday! I give Him the praise Glory and Honor for what is about to take place in my life. I just send up Judah to God right now. This is the day the Lord has made REJOICE and be glad in it. Tell that old Devil, you ain't going nowhere and he will no longer have victory in your situation. God has worked it out and turned it around. VICTORY belongs to the saints of God. Devil we denounce and send you back to the pits of hell from whence you came. You have been messing with God's people long enough as my mother use to say, take your nasty filthy hands on off God's saints. We declare and decree that things are already better for you this day. Walk in your victory, Step, Step, and Step again in your new season! It is right in front of you and it's on the other side of through. I am off work is definitely calling me! Help Me Lord. I am so caught up right now but got to hold my mew just for a few minutes . . . . HERE IT IS BABM PRAISE BREAK take it on now . . . .

Time of Reflections

____

____

____

____

____

August 23

I still got a praise down on the inside of me! Yes, I can't believe that I have been to work for one week. God I thank you that is was a great and peaceful week. I yet give you praise knowing that it is Fantastic Faithful to Believe Friend Friday. Yes, allow this day to be a day that you take time out to tell a friend that you appreciate them for being a friend. Keep in mind the scripture says, in order t . . . o have friends you have a show yourself friendly. A true friend is a priceless gift. You cannot put a price tag on the value of a friendship. Appreciate your friends this day and let them know how much they really mean to you! Someone would love to have the kind of friend you possess in your life. If your friend does not lift you up, and talk about you behind your back, then the chances of that individual is not a friend. If you do not have a friend, then change must take place from within. Everyone need someone to be able to go to and talk to and knowing that they can trust you . . . . GOD Bless You ON This FRIEND FRIDAY!

Time of Reflections

____

____

____

____

____

August 24

I am looking for a Miracle expect the impossible and I feel the intangible and I see the invisible and oh the sky is the limit to what I can have. All you have to do is believe and receive it God will perform it today. Yes, woke up this morning with my mind stayed on Jesus and the song that rang out through my spirit was There is Power In The Name of Jesus to Break Every Chain and to do anything . . . that needs to be done in our lives. We just going to smile and sing our way through this Super Sunny Shining Bright Still Have Joy Saturday! Yes, this joy and peace I have the world didn't give it to me and I refuse to allow the world to take it away. God is up to something great on your behalf. God I just thank you and give you praise for how you are working out things in my life. Through it ALL I learned to trust in Jesus I learn to Trust in God. Cause I am Determined to full fill His Will. Because when I was yet in my mother's womb I was Destined For Purpose for such a time as this. I am going to walk in the Favor of God. Every step I take I am going to take it in the name of Jesus Because Every round goes higher and higher. Thank God that He is My Emmanuel, when I feel like I am by myself, I know I am not because He is with me always and will continually to be with me even to the end of the World. I know without a shout of a doubt that God is MY EVERYTHING. So I praise Him for who He is and what He is going to do in my life today, tomorrow and forever. EXPECT THE GREAT! If you dont want to tell it, then I will tell it what the Lord has done for me . . . . YOU are to been there when He save my soul, you are to been there when He made me whole, He put Joy down in my soul and then He made Me Hold, I never shall forget what He's done for me, You are to been There! Now Run and Tell That, GOD IS GOOD TO ME . . . .

Time of Reflections

August 25

I will lift up my eyes to the hills from whence cometh my help all of my help cometh from the Lord. He will not suffer thy foot to be move, the Lord that keepeth thee He will not slumber or sleep, my help, my help all of my help cometh from the Lord. Today, l just want you to know that your help cometh from the Lord. Thank you Jesus. God is great and greatly to be praised! My hope is in Jesus Christ. Thank God for the past couple of days for giving me the strength and energy that l needed this week to do things l wanted to get done. I have three more major projects to get done and l will be able to relax for a while. I decree and declare that God will pour out His Spirit on each of us this day and whatever needs to be done in your life, He will do just that and l pray even now that He will do something extra special just for you. God blessings just overtake you this day and you will never be the same again! Lord send forth that change we have prayed and talked about release it in the atmosphere this day in Jesus Name it is so.

Time of Reflections

August 26

Well, I know everyone is excited about this Moving Forward to School Marvelous Monday. I just praise God for last night sleeping holy and this morning rising. God is just so good all the times. There is nothing too hard for God. God can do the impossible. Just supply the faith because its already done. Just praise Him while we wait on the manifestation of the Holy Spirit to bring in the results. I know it seem like this is being repeated but I am just following God. Even in the Bible there are times that He said things twice. So I am just encouraging you this morning whoever you are not to give up, not to give in, because you are at the point of your breakthrough. Just a few more rising of the sun you will be on your way into your new season and walking in the newness of life. I just ask God to shield and protect everyone this day, give us the wisdom, patience, and the know how to deal with various things that may arrive. Most important we need to stop and pause and say "LORD HELP ME." Don't allow anything to get to far out there and then ask for His Help but ask for it in the beginning stage and a lot of things we would avoid just by us asking Him to help us in advance. With this in mind, I am starting the chain off to ask Him to Help Us this day, my family, friends, love ones, coworkers, church members, BABM, COGFBJC, Inc as a whole, children, parents, teachers, custodians, cafeteria workers, and WHOSOEVER I did not name. For the Bible said, "Whosoever will let them come." So if you do not see a name or the name bases that you know me on, then the WHOSOEVER will take care of it all. God bless you on this Moving Forward Moving!

Time of Reflections

____

____

____

____

____

August 27

I still got a praise down on the inside. I give God the glory on this terrific thanking God Tuesday. We serve a mighty can do God. It is well with my soul. I hope and trust that this day will go smooth for you as you praise God in the middle of what we may consider a storm of life. Seem like everyday gets better and better as the days go by. Everyday with Jesus gets sweeter and sweeter as the days . . . go by. When things may look like they are out of wack, just know The Father is putting things back together again. It is my prayer and desire that God will just make me over again. He is the potter and l am the clay so Lord just make me and use me as never before as an instrument for your service and glory! Have yourself a terrific thanking Him, telling of His goodness Tuesday . . . .

Time of Reflections

August 28

Good Morning on this Wonderful, Winning Worshipping What Would I do Without Him Wednesday. Yes, I want you all to know that GOD WILL SHOW UP ON TIME. Just when you feel like you needed Him like yesterday year. Jesus is just an on time God. He is so close and near us that when we go through sometimes it is not expedient for Him to intervene. Sometimes He sits back to observe and see what we are going to do and when we cannot seem to get it together or handle the situation the way it suppose to before we start going under, He is there to extend His hand and save us from ALL and ANY situations that may arrive. So don't get disheartened when you feel like He is not coming when you think that you need Him the most. God is a right now God. What take us a life time to get fix and straighten out, He can do it in a 1/2 second. That is the type of God we serve. I want you to know on this Wonderful Winning Wednesday that He is coming to your rescue and you dont have to worry or fret because my GOD HAS AND WILL NEVER EVER FAIL US . . . . Stand on His Word. Good things come to those who wait. So a lot of times David said, I patiently waited on the Lord and He heard my cry and delivered me. So as long as you wait on the Lord, He will come and see about you. Look out He is on His way to take care of you . . . . God loves you this day and everyday and So Do I! God is an Awesome God.

Time of Reflections

August 29

How much more does God has to do to prove that He loves us. For God so loved the world that He gave His only begotten Son, that whosoever believeth in Him shall not perish but have everlasting life. God loved us so much while we were yet sinners He died for us. He proves His love to us over and over again through his grace and mercy. We sing the song well He didn't have to do it but He did. I am so glad He did. I realize that He didn't have to wake me up this morning and start me on my way but I give God praise and Glory because He did it. I just want you to know as you go through this Triumphant, Telling of His Goodness, Trying, and Testing Thursday that God loves you. He loves us so much until He will not put no more on us than we are able to bare. We may think we cannot bare it or had enough of whatever it may be. But God really knows how much we can bare and take. Know that this day whatever comes your way on this trying and testing Thursday that God has already provided away for you to OVERCOME and ESCAPE from it. Be determined don't let no one turn you around or bring you out of Character this day! Keep your feet on solid ground Because you are going to make it. He died in order for us to Make It Through whatever we have to Go Through. Look at it like this, it's only a test that we are going through its going to be over real soon, keep the faith, don't give in, because you are going to win. Be bless in the Lord and know that God loves us so much until He released His angels that have been assigned to us to take care of us this day. Not only did he do that but he allowed Grace and Mercy to follow us through this day. So, I say to you today Don't Worry Be Happy! Smile, You Wear It Well!

Time of Reflections

____

____

____

____

____

August 30

Lord I just want to thank you, Lord I just want to thank You, Lord I just want to thank You, Lord I just want to thank You. I want to thank you for being so good to me; so good to me. YES, Yes, Yes, it is Finally, Faithful to believe, Fantastic, Fun Friday and that is what I am going to have this day. There is no stopping me today. I am so excited and I just can't hide it on this Finally Friday is here. I pray that each of you all are feeling the same way. Knowing God woke us up this morning without any hurt and pain in the body. My day can only go one way and that is up, up, up and way feeling good. Then to top it off, do not have to return to work on Monday! God is just good like that. Do not anyone deter you from being happy or feeling good this morning. One of my BABM Partners was saying how good she was feeling this morning. I know this joy we have this morning the world didn't give it to us and since the world didn't give it to us, we refuse to allow the world to take it away. I know Satan will be waiting somewhere around the corner but I will tell him to get thee behind me this day. The joy of the Lord is my strength. So if you decide you want joy cause nothing is going right you know how I do, I will say leap three times and say Lord, I thank you for giving me joy this day, Lord, I thank you for giving me joy this day, say it like you really mean it LLLLLLOOOOOOOOORRRRRRRDDDDDD, I thank YOOOOOOOOOUUUUUUUUUUUUU for giving me JJJJJJJOOOOOOOYYYYYY this day! Yes, I had to pause and leap myself because I have to be first partaker in what I say and tell people. That felt real good to me. Glory to God! Be bless and know that someone is praying for you. Be careful, Be safe, and I love you (In My Godson; Zious's Voice)!

Time of Reflections

____

____

____

____

____

August 31

Well, I am well rested. Just giving GOD the Glory and praise for all that He has done and for the victory we have won and for the good times and the bad times having you there in my life makes a difference, just having you there. Super Sensational Smiling Sunny Saturday! God has blessed us from Sunday up to this close of a full week. He is worthy of the praise just allow him to bless you this . . . day. When I woke up early in the midnight hour it was a song about Put It All In His Hands. So those who are at the cross road of life and don't know what to do or how to handle that what you are facing with this day, Just Put It In His Hands. He has a plan for your life and that you are bound to see the manifestation of the spirit of God in your life. Even yesterday God begin to speak to me concerning 2014; that it is going to be a year of manifestation in our lives. He is going to manifest some things as never before just look for things to happen and take place. It has already been spoken, decreed and declared and now He must bring the manifestation to the forefront of what is going to be happening in the year of 2014. Well, we are pretty much in September and three months it will be here before you know it. WE have to have the spirit of expectancy. I know I expect my miracle to happen and take place. I just tell God to shake the very foundation of my life and line things up according to His will and plan for my life. I am willing to walk in the plan He has for my life. Yes, I know I am Destined for Purpose on this Super Saturday day and every day! Be bless and remember to put it in His Hands and leave it there. He can work it out and handle it! Step Back and Let God Do It!

Time of Reflections

____

____

____

____

____

Month Nine

SEPTEMBER

September 1

Moving Forward, Making the Right Choices Monday! I am getting myself together cause I got some place to go and I am praying when I get there I see everyone I know, I wanna go to Heaven. That's the Place for Me. Just knowing that today is Monday and I am going to give God what is due to him that is all that matters. I just desire that closer walk with Him. The song writer wrote, How many times do we go against your will but you forgive us and never turn and walk away, but yet I still hear you calling my name. Yes, I want you to know that He is yet calling for me, you, you, and you today. He said my sheep hears my voice. The Lord is my Shepard. You said, you are my shepard why aren't you following me. If He is your shepard this day, please allow Him to lead you and you follow Him where He is trying to take you and get you to go. I love that song. These songs have just being with me this morning and I give Him the glory and praise. Allow those words to bless you this morning as you get ready to go to the house of God and get your praise on. I give God the glory for the expectations I have on this day. I expect the great and mighty move of God in HIS FULLNESS. Don't hold back on GOD, because He did not hold back on you this morning. If your church praise Him, and My Church Praise Him, there should be enough praises going on to shake heaven until the blessings begin to fall and overshadow us. When Praises GO Up, The Blessings Come Down! Are yours falling down?

Time of Reflections

September 2

Listening at the storm last night along with the sound of the rain; I can't help but say, I can hear the abundance! Then to go along with the storm, "Though the storms keep on raging in our lives and sometimes it's hard to tell the night from day, but still that hope that lies within is reassure as I keep my eyes upon the blessed shore I Know He'll lead me safely to that blessed place He has prepared. But if the storms don't cease and just in case the wind keeps on blowing in our lives our souls have been anchored in the Lord! On this taking it to Jesus, Trusting in him Tuesday just know that our souls must be anchored in the Lord. Things are going to come and things are going to go but we must keep our focus on Christ. On Christ the solid rock I stand all other ground is sink and sand. So as you go out this day, press forward there is no other way for us to go but FORWARD and UP. Thank God for just being so good and Master of it all. It is my prayer that God will help all of us this day and know there is nothing to hard for God and if He has done it before He will and can do it AGAIN! Be encouraged my family, brothers and sisters!

Time of Reflections

___

___

___

___

___

September 3

How Great Is our God on this Wonderful, Waiting on Jesus Wednesday! I just feel good down in my soul. I felt like dancing 4:00 this morning. Oh just when I think of the Goodness of Jesus and all that He has done for me; my soul cries out Glory, I thank God for saving me. Right now my joy is sweet and my soul is complete that's why I'm save by his power divine. Just think of something that God has done to allow you to know just how Great He Is! Then just give Him praise for that. If you really want to move God today, well you can move Him through your praise. In spite of what is going on around us, we can just look at all God's Creation and be thankful to be able just to see it. Most things God called into being but when it came to us HE CREATED US IN HIS IMAGE. So we are yet bless. He took his own precious time and made us just like Him. I just want you to join in with me this Worshipping Him Wednesday and just thank Him for 1) Who He Is, 2) For the things that He has done, 3) For what He is doing even now, and 4) A praise in advance For what He is getting ready to do. I believe God! I am determined no matter what come or go this way, I refuse to lose Hope In God. There is Hope In God. One thing about it when the devil says no, God says YES! So Who are you going to listen to this day. I shall listen and believe the report of the Lord. One, Two, Get Ready and Help Me a Praise Him!

Time of Reflections

____

____

____

____

____

September 4

I love you Jesus, I worship and adore you, Just want to tell you that I love you more than anything! Yes, on this way in the mist of it all Triumphant, Take me Back, Through thick and thin Thursday, I pray that it will be a great day for each of you. I pray God face shine upon each of us as we go through this day. There is nothing too hard for God. I just thank God for being able to sleep and get some sound sleep last night. Then I just thank God for this morning rising, closed in my right mind, have the use and activity of my limbs and pain free it is just a blessing. I can walk and talk, see and hear. We just don't know how bless we are. I give God praise and Glory this day. We will be praying and interceding on your behalf that God will work some things out, shake some things out, smooth some things out, and just do what He wants to do in your life by ruling and super ruling in every aspect and situation. I believe God with you that it is already done. I want to go Higher, Higher than I ever been before in Him! Please take and set aside some time today just to worship Him by singing a song of melody within your heart. I guess I will start it off, Let The Glory of The Lord Rise Among Us, Let the Praises of Our King Rise Among Us, Oh Oh Oh, Let It Rise! Be forever Bless!

Time of Reflections

September 5

Wow, Slept so good last night but still the joy bells are yet ringing down in my soul on this Fret not, Forgiven, Faithful to Believe Friday! The Lord spoke to be and shared with me sometimes things are not what it looks like. But we have to press through it all. The song that is ringing down in my soul "MY GREATER IS COMING" I begin to talk in the atmosphere that whatever is holding my Greater back I declare and decree right now that the Holy Spirit would allow it to be released even this day! Oh God oh what joy has flood my soul this morning something happen and now right now I know He touched, Demonn this morning and He made me whole. Oh yes, HE is willing and able to do it for and to you as well. I Touch and agree not being a selfish person that your Greater will come as well. WE have been in our season of waiting and anticipation but our season of receiving our GREATER is around the corner. I encourage you this morning not to be weary in well doing for in due season WE are going to REAP OUR GREATER if we faint not! WE must abide in the Word of God and He must abide in us and we can ask what we want and desire and He will do it for us. GOD is not a man that He should lie, and I know for a fact His Word is True and Will Remain True so I expect nothing less but "MY GREATER" To be manifested and come to pass in my life. When you know there is something in the mail coming for you, you have that excitement and go to the mailbox to check to see if it arrived. You didn't see it that day but you go back the next day and the next and eventually it came. So you maybe like country boy what are you talking about. I am saying LOOK for it, if it doesn't come today, nor tomorrow I know that IT WILL COME. Though it Tarry We Must Wait On It, Because OUR GREATER IS COMING. Be Bless This Day and just move your head to the right a little bit like you are peeping around the corner and See Do You See Your Greater. Then Look to the Left to see if you see your GREATER. Keep Looking because I know for a fact it is on the Way. You Can Take This TO The Bank and Bank On It.! YOUR GREATER IS COMING. MY GREATER IS COMING! If He Done It Before He Can Do It Again.

Time of Reflections

____

____

____

____

____

September 6

I am so bless this Super, Standing Still, Holding On Saturday! I hope and trust that all is yet well with you and that you have had a bless week. If things went kind of up and down for you, I hope this day will be a smooth sailing day for you! Just count it all JOY no matter what. Just knowing that today is Friday is enough to give GOD praise. Rejoice in the Lord and again I say Rejoice. This is the day the Lord has made, I will rejoice and be glad in it. I pray that God will give you a special peace that surpasseth all understanding. You are my peace, you are my peace, you are my peace and I worship you. You have delivered my soul from the spare of the enemy. In the mist of my storm you held and protected me, you are my peace, you are my peace, you are my peace and I worship you! Yes, Jesus said, I give you peace not as the world giveth. John 14:27 Peace I leave with you, my peace I give unto you: not as the world giveth, give I unto you. Let not your heart be troubled, neither let it be afraid. Just allow His peace to bless you on this day. Despite of what you are going through and what it looks like right now just reach out and grab hold to HIS PEACE. That is the word and thought of today PEACE . . . .

Every time God sends blessings the devil has to mess. But I refuse to Break, I will bend, talking to the Lord above. I got the victory praise the Lord. Oh I got, I got the victory praise the Lord Holy Ghost abiding way down in my soul, I got the victory praise the Lord.

Time of Reflections

____

____

____

____

____

September 7

Well, let me get my day started. I was thinking that it would be a Serving the Lord, Shaking the devil off Sunday! If we do not move forward then nothing will get done. So as you go through this day, even in my still quiet hour. I was able to allow devotion to my Lord and Savior. Me and Andrea Crouch had a time up in the house singing praises to the Lord. I took it back ole school. . . ."TAKE ME BACK TO THE PLACE WHERE I FIRST BELIEVE YOU" I couldn't stop praising the Lord while God presence was just blessing me this morning. Sometimes we need to go back to the place when we first God saved and allow that same power, zeal and fire to take charge in our right now situation. That is my prayer Lord allow me to go back to the place where I first believe you. WE still need that passion that we had back then for now to keep pressing forward. We get comfortable and relaxed on this journey and that is what allows the enemy to attack because the zeal is sleep. But I will bless the Lord at all times and His praises shall continually be in my mouth. So we just tell the Lord to Fill us up again and allow our cups to overflow and RESTORE UNTO US THE JOY THAT WE ONCE HAD, THE POWER & ZEAL WE Had. HE can stir it up within us even now. So as you go through this day, just ask God to take you back spiritually to the place once you told Him Yes and When You Accepted Him as Lord and Savior of your life. God bless you all this day. KNOW THIS ONE THING "IT'S NOT OVER UNTIL GOD SAYS IT'S OVER!"

Time of Reflections

____

____

____

____

____

September 8

Good Monday Morning to each of you! I pray this will be a Moving Forward, SON Filled, Saying Yes To His Will, Monday! God is up to something great on this day. We have to allow ourselves to get into this presence. In His presence is fullness of Joy! Where the spirit of the Lord is there is Liberty. So if you want to be set free and delivered, I encourage each of us to get into His presence. God is able and willing to set you (THE CAPTIVE) Free on this day. No longer will you have to be entangled with the yoke of bondage but you can be free. And who the Son sets Free is Free in Deed. Why don't you allow Him to free you this day from whatever it is that is holding you back from MOVING FORWARD in His Will and the plan that he has set for your life. Just step out in faith on today because it's all about what you want this day. He can and will do it for us. It's time to let it go so we can advance the kingdom of God. We need to be Kingdome Builders so those that are lost will not have to be lost anymore. Just Step into your Freedom while the water is trouble on this day. God really wants to do it for you this day. You are so special to Him and you mean a lot to Him. Despite what others say and think; one thing for sure Jesus died just for you. That is how much He really loves YOU! Be blessed this day and allow God to set you Free. I am free praise the Lord I am free, no longer bound, no more chains holding me, my soul is resting it's just a blessing praise the Lord Hallelujah I am Free . . . .

Time of Reflections

____

____

____

____

____

September 9

Thanking God for a wonderful morning and I know that I will look to the hills from whence cometh my help because all of my help comes from the Lord! I give God the glory what He is doing in my life. There is a shaking in the atmosphere and I realize whatever the devil meant for my bad, I decree and declare that God has changed it around for my good. I know what God says about me and that is all . . . that counts and matters. On this journey I want to know that I have pleased God in my doings. The song said, I will go if I have to go by myself but I am Determined to get to heaven. If you desire not to go, then don't hinder me. My mind is made up, I am on my way up and I am going on with the Lord. So on this Turning it around, Trusting in him Tuesday, just purpose in your heart that you want to please the Lord, through your walk and your talk on this day. Just think for a second whatever comes up, ask yourself, What Would JESUS DO or How WOULD JESUS RESPOND. Allow Him to lead and guide you this day as he direct your footsteps to carry out the plan He has for your life. God bless each of you. I thank God for the ones who share their testimony about what God is doing in your life through these encouraging and motivational thoughts. Keep looking up to God, because the prayers of the righteous availeth much. When I say I pray for you, that is what I do even when I should be asleep, I am interceding on your behalf that God will move as never before. Give Him the Glory.

Time of Reflections

____

____

____

____

____

September 10

Thanking God for this Telling Satan I don't belong to him, telling Satan to back off, Waiting On Jesus, Wonderful, Work it Out Wednesday! Yes, this is the day the Lord has made I will rejoice and be glad in it. Yes, I am getting better all the times. I am not where I want to be but Lord I am striving, and I thank God I am not where I use to be because of His Grace and Mercy that allowed me to Move Forward in Him. God is so awesome. WE say it time and time again but have we just really stop to reflect on His goodness. When we don't cross every t and dot every i, He looks beyond all our faults and He sees our needs. But my God shall supply all of your needs according to His riches in glory. Whatever needs you have today know that God has taken care of them. Not only does He supplies our needs, but He goes beyond that. If we delight ourselves in Him, then He will give us the desires of our hearts. What is your heart desiring this day? If it is in the will of God, that desire is going to be fulfill so according to your faith be it done unto you. God is great and greatly to be praised. So just thank God on this Terrific Tuesday for the needs He has supplied in your life; then give Him an advance praise for the desires of your heart been fulfilled. I touch and agree with you this day as I declare and decree in your life that every need will be supplied and that you will not go lacking for anything. After all your needs are met, I pray that God would give you extra. My cup runneth over surely goodness and mercy shall follow me all the days of my life and I will well in the house of the Lord. In other words, I want you to know that I can hear the abundance of Rain and that the OVERFLOW is on the way! Trust and believe God this Wonderful Wednesday. Be Forever Bless!

Time of Reflections

____

____

____

____

____

September 11

Yes, Yes, Yes, It is the day after the hump day! Giving glory and honor to GOD for allowing us this Through thick and thin, Trampling over the enemy, Triumphant Thursday. Yes, we were able to get quiet a few praises in on this morning. God is yet in the blessing business. I want you all to know that Prayer Changes Things, People and Situations. Prayer is the Key and Faith unlocks the door. When was the last time you really spent time praying, talking and seeking the face of God? The prayers of the righteous availeth much. Don't be dismay whatever betides you because God will take care of you. Just Pray Until Something Happen. As you go through this day just pray and intercede on the behalf of others and also take time to pray for yourself. If you believe God for others and that what you are praying for them will happen, then God will allow whatever you pray for to happen for you. Release your faith this day. That thing that you prayed for and you feel God has not answered it; then I encourage you this day to go back and pray that prayer again. God has not forgotten about you. What seems impossible to man, once you give it to God, you will know with God all things are possible if you only believe. What are you believing God today for in your life. God still answers prayer. He is yet a prayer answering God and God is not slack concerning His promises but He is able to fulfill everyone of them. I stand on His Word, which says, if you abide in me and I abide in you; then you can ask anything in my name and I will do it. So Here I come to you this day as I abide in you and you abide in me and I make my request known unto you this day, and not only me but my family, friends, love ones, TP&D, BABM, & COGFBJC, Inc. and I pray God that you will do something great, special, and mightily on their behalf. GOD I pray that you send a right now miracle and a right now change in our situations. God just give us that assurance this day that it is so and it is done in your name. God those that are waiting to actually see the results of their request, God make it known to them this day. It is my prayer God that you will do it even now and work it out on their behalf. WE stand on your Word and we supply the faith that is needed this day for you to answer our prayer, plea, and request. God we declare it and we decree it right now whoever reads this you do it for them and we will not wait for the manifestation but we will praise you right now in Jesus Name. GO AHEAD, I am not beside you but lift your hands and look towards Heaven and give God some praise for working it out for you this day! AMEN.

Time of Reflections

____

____

____

____

____

September 12

I will bless thee oh Lord on this Faithful to Believe Friday! I am praising God that things are well as they are. When your feet hit the floor and after getting a good night sleep and there is no pain in the body that is a blessing. I feel good this morning and I know there is nothing going to happen or take place in my life this day that God and I cannot handle. If it comes to me, then God is going to take me by the hand and walk, take, or tote me through it. I just believe God the more for what He is doing. The more you love on Him and trust in Him and take Him at His Word; then there is nothing He want do to prove how much He loves and cares for those who diligently seek after Him. When you go through and do not know what to do, stand still, rest in Him, rely on Him and ask Him to HELP YOU each and every day of your life. We have not because we ask not. It doesn't matter how often you need to stop on this day and SAY LORD HELP ME THROUGH THIS DAY! I know that He will do it for you. WE have to continue to be steadfast, unmoveable, always abounding in the work of the Lord for as much as we know our Labor is not in vain. This day do not be moved by your situation or come out of character because of what you are going through but allow you character to change that situation by counting it all joy. Let me share this scripture with you Psalms 37:1-9: Fret not thyself because of evildoers, neither be thou envious against the workers of iniquity.

2 For they shall soon be cut down like the grass, and wither as the green herb. 3 Trust in the Lord, and do good; so shalt thou dwell in the land, and verily thou shalt be fed. 4 Delight thyself also in the Lord: and he shall give thee the desires of thine heart. 5 Commit thy way unto the Lord; trust also in him; and he shall bring it to pass. 6 And he shall bring forth thy righteousness as the light, and thy judgment as the noonday. 7 Rest in the Lord, and wait patiently for him: fret not thyself because of him who prospereth in his way, because of the man who bringeth wicked devices to pass. 8 Cease from anger, and forsake wrath: fret not thyself in any wise to do evil. 9 For evildoers shall be cut off: but those that wait upon the Lord, they shall inherit the earth.

When things get just a little rocky or shaky today just remember not to Fret but trust in Him who will deliver you out victoriously. God bless you and know that God and I love you!

Time of Reflections

___

___

___

___

___

September 13

This little light of mine, I am going to let it shine everywhere I go. As we go through this Stepping on the Devil's Head Saturday, be sure to let your light shine. Your life is the only BIBLE that people would ever open and read. If you are not displaying God or a positive character, then you will turn them to follow something else. Make sure we live a life that is pleasing to God on a daily basis. The more we walk in His will and way, the better off we will be in the end. He reigns forever, He reigns forever and ever more! Keep Christ in your heart and all that you do acknowledge Him in all your ways and He will direct our paths.

Time of Reflections

____

____

____

____

____

September 14

It's Sunday morning we must to the church. God has yet been good to us all and even at this busy day, we must yet give God some praises for the things in which He has done, doing and yet going to do! There's no God like Jehovah! You can search here and there but you will never find no one like Him. What a true saying this morning, that Can't Nobody do Me Like Jesus, because He's My Friend. Thank God for Being my friend. I just praise Him. The song that had me up all night just about was the only thing I could say, God My Savior, God My Healer, God My Deliverer, Yes He Is. Then this morning I was able to get the first part of the song. Every Praise is to Our God! That works for me and I am going to give Him what is due to Him. He made it possible for me to get up this morning clothed in my right mind. So I am just on my praise this morning. I hope and trust that each of you have a great day and know God is still on the throne. Be bless!

Time of Reflections

____

____

____

____

____

An Extra Reading

Take it there now this morning: I love You Jesus, I Worship and Adore You, Just Want To Tell You That I Love You More Than Anything. Yes, I love Him this beautiful Sunnshine, Singing, Smiling, Saying yes to His Will, Sensational Sunday! I am just in my praise mood once again. Tell Jesus How Much I Love Him More Than Anything. Forsake all others and put Jesus number one in your life. We have to deny yourself and follow Him. I am just excited about this last fiscal day in this year for us. I expect a mighty move of GOD and yes there is a WORD from the Lord so walk through the Doors of Total Praise & Deliverance and allow the Holy Spirit to Rest Upon you this day! God is great and greatly to be praised. I am not going to ask God for nothing this day for us but I just want you to help me Praise & Thank Him This morning for who He is and for whose we are. Come on start clapping those hands even now. When the devil hear us clapping our hands unto the Lord, he gets mad and upset and cover up his ears. Let us help him keep his ears closed this day as we Praise and Worship the Most High God. Let Everything that Has Breath Praise the Lord. Let Every Church This Day Be Filled With Praise. I Want to hear every COGFBJC, Inc, BABM, and all churches in the surrounding areas. I know I will hear TP&D cause I will be in the house getting my praise on what about you? Be Bless and Turn Up The Volume once again as I check out of here, I love you Jesus, I worship and Adore you, just want to tell you that I love you, more than anything . . . . More than anything, more than anything!

"I AM COMING OUT" is selling real good. God is truly blessing and touching the hearts of individual to purchase their book. He also have great people helping them to sale. I am just thankful for what God is doing in this hour! This is a book that will change your life and encourage your life the more . . . . Thanks once again for everyone's support and prayers in this endeavor. May God bless each of you all real, real good! To the Zionites, I want to be able to sleep and rest tonight! I want to know how can you all have a "COMING OUT PARTY WITHOUT ME?" Smiling . . . . The AUTHOR SHOULD HAVE BEEN THERE . . . . As my friend sings, You Are To Been There . . . I should've been there! I am so happy right now. But after everything is over there will be another Coming Out Party & Book Signing Soon. Stay Tuned!

September 15

This is another day and the start of a new work week! I pray this day will get better and better each minute. On this Marvelous, Miracle Working, Moving Forward Monday. Sometimes we just have to stop, drop, and think. Get back up and keep moving forward. On this road we call life is full of knocks and bruises, but we have to stop and look to the Hills From Whence Cometh Our Help. Then we have to drop down on our knees and ask God to Help Us. Even in the last process we have to think and ask Jesus, What Would Jesus Do? When He give you the answer then we must follow through with it. After He talks to you and you "CAST ALL YOUR CARES ON HIM" Then move forward. Some things are not meant to be and we just have to say, Lord Help Me to Accept What God Allows! So as you move forward this marvelous, miracle moment Monday, just Stop, Drop, and Think and Move Forward. God has a plan for our lives sometimes we may can't see it or understand it but we will by and by. WE must be determined to stay in His Will no matter what. As I close this morning, remember the safest place in the whole wide world is in the WILL OF GOD! If you are not in His will today, please get in His Will so you can move forward for the plan He has for your life. Be bless and Somebody Pray for Me This Day! Everytime you think about me just tell God all about it!

Time of Reflections

____
____
____
____
____

September 16

I am feeling mighty happy, feeling mighty fine, yes I am enjoying Jesus Hallelujah! Good morning everyone, I hope and trust that all is well with you on this Taking It TO The Next Level, Trusting Him, Telling Satan To Get The Behind, Telling His Goodness, Testifying, Terrific, Taking one day at a time, Tuesday. The Joy of the Lord is my strength. I just feel such a peace and calmness this morning. Know this one thing that God is working it out for you, you and especially you. Today make up in your mind that you are going to be happy all day long. Do not let nothing or no one take that away from you. The joy that I have the world didn't give it to me and please the world can't take it away. God is allowing you to Move Forward for a reason and the only way we can go and have good results is Forward/ UP To The Next Level in Him. God is up to something great for you my brothers, sisters, friends, love ones, TP&D, MT. Zion, COGFBJC, BABM, & #2! Just allow Him to lead and guide you in the right direction. On this road you may have speed bumps, slow down, u-turn or detours, but trust in Him that He is going to take you there. Follow Jesus, take no chance of getting lost, follow Jesus, He has a plan to take you to the top, and if He doesn't there is no one else who can. So allow Him to take you up higher and higher than you have ever been before. I feel so good this day until I am on My Way Up to My Next Level. If you don't want to go, then don't Hinder Me. Anybody standing around the spiritual elevator. Well, I am holding the door for you so if you going to the up floor, through the spiritual eye step on and let us go up together. God bless you this terrific Tuesday! My Greater Is Coming! I don't want to be selfish, OUR GREATER IS COMING!

Time of Reflections

____

____

____

____

____

September 17

Praising God for this New Day in which He allowed us to see. God is yet in the blessing business. He is yet opening doors, making ways, turning things around and doing what He does best. Just keep providing for us and blessing us over and over again. We are half way there to see a close of another week. Wonderful, working, worshipping, winning, why I love Him so Much Wednesday! Be encouraged this day and hang on in there. God has truly got you covered. You are not alone. God said He will be with us even until the end of the world. So as you take one day at a time and one step at a time know He is there by our side. I haven't had trouble with my computer in a long time but Satan is saying it's time for him to intercept this message but he is a liar and the father of lies. This message will go out and accomplish what it supposes to do this day. Just worship God this day in the beauty of Holiness.

Time of Reflections

____

____

____

____

____

September 18

Good morning everyone! The joy bells are yet ringing down in my sanctified soul. Yes, it is Triumph Telling of His Goodness, Trusting in Him, Trying to encourage somebody, thanking Him Thursday! Yes, allow the grace of God to shine upon you this day as you tell of His goodness, we must continue to trust in Him. The song says I will trust in the Lord until I die. Once we do that and have given our life over to Him, that puts us in Heaven Bound Status! Yes, God wants it all today, He wants it all today. Love me with your whole heart, He wants it all today! Know as you go through this day telling others how good He is just know that we must give Him our all today on this beautiful Thursday! Feel free to add a line to the song, I admit, I don't know it all but I do know He wants it All Today! Since He wants it all today, make sure He gets it all from you this day! God bless be encouraged and move forward there are higher heights and deeper depths.

Time of Reflections

September 19

Fantastic, Feeling Good, Faithful to believe, Following after Him Friday! Don't have much to say this day but I am feeling happy and thanking God for all the blessings He have stored upon me. You don't know like I know what the Lord has done for me. I am going to get my praise on this day and magnify the God of my salvation. I hope and trust that the joy that I am feeling will enter into my computer and come out of your computer while you are reading this. As you go through this day just think and tell yourself that CANT NOBODY DO ME LIKE JESUS, CANT NOBODY DO ME LIKE THE LORD. You can search all over here and there but you will never ever find no one GREATER THAN HIM (GOD)! Enjoy your day and just keep your hands in His hands and everything will be alright!

Time of Reflections

____

____

____

____

____

September 20

Praising God for another day. Enjoy your day in which the Lord hath made. I am going to rejoice because of this super sensational Saturday! I have something to praise the Lord for; He brought me out of darkness into the marvelous light I have something to praise the Lord for. Reflect on his goodness this Shaking the devil off, Somebody Prayed for Me Super Saturday.

Time of Reflections

____

____

____

____

____

September 21

Yes, praising God for another Still Holding On, Stepping On, Spirit Fall On Me Sunday! If it had not been for the Lord on my side where would I be? I am Enjoying being back home once again. I searched and went here and there and I found there is no place like home. I hope and trust each of you had a great day and know God is yet in the blessing business. When I just think of the goodness of Jesus and all He has done for me my soul cries out Hallelujah I thank God for Saving Me! Be bless and will meet you here in the morning.

Time of Reflections

____

____

____

____

____

September 22

Yet praising the God of my Salvation. This is my story, this is my song, Praising My Savior All the Day Long! I went to bed early last night to allow this body to get the proper rest that it needed from this past week. I got up feeling mighty happy. Yes, I had to sing "EVERY PRAISE IS TO OUR GOD" And I give Him all the praise glory and honor on this Moving Forward, Making Money, Marvelous, Miracle Monday. Just help me give every praise to My God this Morning. I just need two or three people to touch and agree with me this morning and just lift Him up. I feel a praise break early this morning. Throughout this day, if you feel like things are getting to overwhelming just feel free to shout with me "GLORY" Go head and practice it right now, Shout "Glory", say it again Shout Glory; Say it like you really mean it and that something is getting ready to happen or your break through has arrived. Say it one more time "GLORYRRRRRRRYYYYYYYYYYYYY" Be forever blessed my friends and family, love ones, TP&D, BABM & COGFBJC, Inc. If you feel left out I am referring to you too. Much love here!

Time of Reflections

____

____

____

____

____

September 23

Take Me to The King on This Terrific, Testifying, Thanking God Tuesday. If you take me before the king on this day, then I know that everything will be alright. Lord it's in your hands, Lord it's in your hands this day I put it in your hands. As we go through out this day, we must learn to give whatever it is to Jesus and allow Him to work it out. We may wonder how things are the way they are and why things are the way they are but know that God has a plan for your life and He is just allowing things to line up the way that He wants to so that He can move and take you to another level in him. I once heard my Pastor say, when you go into your new season or dimension there are some folks that are not able to go with you into it! So just shake it off and keep on pressing for higher ground. There is something at the end waiting for you. I am not talking about life end, but at the end of your through there is something that awaits you. If God brings you to it, then He is the only one that will get you through it. So life up Holy Hands and Move Forward in Him cause we are Destined For A Divine Purpose! Be bless this day and be encouraged no matter what you going through, He got the answer for you, trust and obey, and the answer will come through for you! You wanted a sign and God is sending you that sign that you are wanting and looking for in order for you to get confirmation on what He is doing and going to do for you! Be forever bless . . .

Time of Reflections

____

____

____

____

____

September 24

Well today the enemy did not want me to post. On this halfway point of the week I am more DETERMINE TO Defeat him. So I have victory over every circumstance and situation. I give God the glory and praise. He is yet turning things around for us. It may seem like it's taking a pretty good while but hold on and hold out and you will see the manifestation of God working it out for you. On this wonder waiting on Him, worshipping, working, winning, willing to do His will Wednesday. You continue to press forward as never before. Be determine to make it through this day. The word you should be saying is I am Determined! I touch and agree as you are determined to be healed, delivered, and set free this day problems, trouble and situations throw it on the Master and let Him handle it.

Time of Reflections

____

____

____

____

____

September 25

Today is Taking it to Jesus, Turning it around, Triumphant Thursday! We always look for the best of the best to come our way but it never reaches its destination. Here I am to worship, here I am to bow down, here I am to say that you're my God. We live in various seasons and when they end you will know it. I am moving forward wherever this journey we call life leads me then that is where I will follow. I am stopping, dropping, and rolling on to another place and venture in God. No use nobody trying to turn me around for my heart is fixed and my mind is made up ain't no use nobody trying to turn me around. Dead End doesn't mean it's the end take another route and you will get were God wants you to be. Have a triumphant telling Jesus all about it Thursday. I know GOD has real people that prayed and interceded on my behalf today. Praise God for true and real soldiers!

Time of Reflections

____

____

____

____

____

September 26

Faithful to believe Friday is here! Oh how l love this day. Nothing else matter but Go and how he is going to see me through this day. God always know what we need and when we need it. I wouldn't serve no other God but him. If your God is not working for you, then try mine. How l love Jesus because He first loves me. Think about this on this faithful to believe Friday and love on him the more. God bless each of you this day.

Time of Reflections

____

____

____

____

____

September 27

Still holding on, staying in my lane Saturday. Giving glory to the most high God for who He is and doing in my life. We have to keep or hands in the master hands and keep moving forward! God has always stood by my side he has always been my guide when my friends walk away and turn back on me He stood right by my side. As you go through this day know that He is standing by your side. Enjoy Jesus this day.

Time of Reflections

____

____

____

____

____

September 28

Praise the Lord Everybody! Yes this is my story this is my song praising my savior all the day long. I am so grateful how God continues to make and mold me how and what he wants me to be. I am wiser and stronger because of Him. I love him more than anything it is Him God who makes my life complete. Off to church l go Satan get out my way because God and l are going to drive you over the edge and back to hell. Saints enjoy your day and put God first in all that you do and it will save us a lot of headache and pain. I am yet Standing on a Sure Foundation, Somebody had me on their mind Sunday.

Time of Reflections

____

____

____

____

____

September 29

What a wonderful day in the neighborhood! I expect blessings this Moving Forward Marvelous making me clean inside Monday. The song that l think about is what can wash away my sins nothing but the blood of Jesus. Whatever spots maybe in our lives the gain, tide or shout just want work. We have to allow His blood to do the cleaning. As he cleans us we will be pure and clean from the inside out. God is still in control of my life. As we go through this day let us take our spiritual baths and allow him to clean us up the way he wants to do it.

Time of Reflections

____

____

____

____

____

September 30

As we close out the last day of this month, I want to clap my hands a little louder than before, l want to scream louder than before, l want to turn wider than before. Freedom, freedom, freedom, freedom. With all this going on right now this is a thanking God, trusting in Him, telling of his goodness Tuesday. God is worthy of all the praise. When you forget about yourself and issues then you can focus more on God. I have learned to put all my trust in Jesus because He is the one to make everything alright. Be bless this day and know there is Hope in God!

Time of Reflections

Month Ten

OCTOBER

October 1

What away to start off this 10th month with a worshipping, waiting on him to deliver, working Wednesday. I am encouraged and more determined to walk with Jesus yes I am. WE have to be determined to allow Christ to be our everything as we walk in and by his Word. In the Word of God we do have a hiding place. I will bless thee oh Lord this halfway point that he has taken care of us. It is well with my soul. Take time to worship him were ever you are in your life. Yes, if you want him to move, I dare you to praise and worship him this day. Keep looking up and moving forward to the King. Watch God we work some things out for you this day. It's not over until God says it's over. Be forever bless!

Time of Reflections

____

____

____

____

____

October 2

Lord lift us up this triumphant Thursday where we belong, where the eagles fly on the mountain high. If we stay on that spiritual high it's hard for Satan to get to us. Stay out of Satan territory. He will fool you and have you thinking opposite of the way things really are. Don't allow Satan to attack your mind' once he gets your mind then he will eventually get all of you. Tell that old devil you may bend but you refuse to break. Be encouraged and keep looking to Jesus the Author and Finisher of our faith.

Time of Reflections

____

____

____

____

____

October 3

Final Friday is here so we must Fret Not because of Evildoers and Follow after him. Just need 30 more minutes but got to be up and moving forward this day. Don't put off for tomorrow what you know you can do today. As Nike symbol stands for "Just Do It" and once you get it done you will be so glad you did. Enjoy this day and get done what you need to get done. God bless each of you.

Time of Reflections

October 4

We sing the praises to our King on this super sunny feeling good Saturday. There is a lot to be done so we must get out our to do list and rise to get it done. First thing on this to do list is put God first and everything else will fall in place. It is a praying time and we must pray ye one for another. My mind is made up and l am determined to walk and follow Jesus yes l am. We need to pray for the government that the chains be broken and loose so people can get on with their lives. It could be us affected but since it's not this time let us roll a ball of prayer for those who are. God bless you all once again.

Time of Reflections

October 5

It's save by his power divine, singing, smiling, saying yes to his will Sunday. There is an out pouring of God's spirit coming your way. Just yield yourself for his purpose and will. God is up to something great. Keep expecting looking and believing cause it is coming to pass. I will not let him go this day until he blesses my soul. Speak Lord for your servant heareth and here am I Lord. Don't hold back your praises because God didn't hold back his blessings concerning you.

Time of Reflections

____

____

____

____

____

October 6

All that l am and hope to be on this moving forward expecting miracle Monday I am fully committed to his will and to his way. God is yet blessing us over and over again. I am where I am because of him. Each and every day I am stronger and wiser sometimes people want to play mind games to see what you are going to do but I am determined to yet stand. There is an Urgency for us to get to the King. In his presence is fullness of joy. Be encouraged and stay in his image and presence today. Don't let know one pull you out of character be bless this marvelous Monday.

Time of Reflections

____

____

____

____

____

October 7

Well, I cannot remember the song that was ringing in my ears all night and morning. But one thing about it, I would just say Melodies From Heaven Rain Down on US this Terrific, Telling of His Goodness, To Close to Turn Around Tuesday! God is not through pouring out his blessings and spirit upon us. WE must stay in the right position and be in tuned to hear the voice of God so we can stay continually in his will. God is yet doing great things on this day and know that someone is yet praying for you this day. Yes, they had you on their mind and they took this time to pray for you. Be bless and tell someone of God Goodness in the past 8 minutes. WE do not have to go back 24 hours to know how Good God really is. Since it is 10/8/13 lets reflect on his goodness for the past 8 minutes . . . . Don't Worry Be Happy!

Time of Reflections

____

____

____

____

____

October 8

Yes, You don't know my story or the things that I been through, you don't know my pain or what I had to go through to get here, don't try to figure it out but my worship on this winning, waiting on God, working, wonderful Wednesday, is for real. I give God the praise for all that he is yet doing. He has blessed us to get through this half way point of this week. Time is yet moving forward. As time move forward, I want to continue to move forward the more in his will. Know this day that God is yet concerned about you and he is working it out for you. It may not feel good what you are going through, may not even look good what you are facing but know this one thing, when He brings you out, you will come through as pure Gold. Then you can say, "How I Got Over, How I Got Over, My Soul Looks Back and Wonder How I Got Over." This too shall pass. Take some time on this day and just go into a worship mood before entering into the work place and see want you have a better or GREATER DAY! Yes, Your Greater Is Yet Around The Corner. Don't give up God has a plan for your life and after you done all that you know to do and dont know what else to do, JUST KEEP STANDING UNTIL YOUR HELP GETS THERE! YOUR HELP IS ON THE WAY!

Time of Reflections

____

____

____

____

____

October 9

It's another day and I give God all the praises for allowing me to just embrace it with love, joy, peace, and happiness. I am so grateful for this Triumphant, Thanking Him, Turning it around Thursday. I feel good down on the inside this morning. God is truly and definitely MY EVERYTHING. As good as GOD has been to us we cannot afford not to praise his name. Let Us Send A Praise Blast To GOD this day. Just think of the goodness of Jesus and all that He has done, what he is doing now, and what he is going to do for you and send a praise blast into the atmosphere. Each and every day God is doing something for each of us. It is not all about the finance that he blesses us with but if he sends a word via person, text, email, mail, telephone that is going to inspire, encourage, or motivate us to make it through one more day, then God has done for us that day what needed to be done. I will be the first to send the praise blast into heaven what word or praise are you sending to him this day! I shout GLORY, GLORY, GLORY! LORD YOU ARE SO WORTHY and I GIVE YOU ALL THE PRAISE EVEN NOW . . . . GLORY, GLORY, GLOOOOOORRRRRRRRYYYYYYYY! Send your Praise Blast to God This Day!

Time of Reflections

____

____

____

____

____

October 10

Following God, Faithful to believe, Feeling Good Friday is Finally here. Let the earth rejoice. I know this is the day the Lord has made I am going to rejoice and be glad in it. Nothing is going to happen this day that God is not going to bring me through. I feel good down in my soul. I just thank God that he knows what to do, when to do, and most important how to do things that will work out for our good. We speak a lot of positive things but we have to supply the faith in order for it to happen. What the devil means for your bad God is a turning it around God for your good! What a mighty God we serve angels bow before him, heaven and earth adore what a mighty God we serve! So as you go through this feeling good Friday, just think what type of Good you serve.

Time of Reflections

____

____

____

____

____

October 11

Its Super Football Saturday and those 1st thru 4th graders will be ready. It is so amazing to take out time with these young people. This is a good way to show them positive things so they would not get into trouble. Trouble and evil is all around but if we do not show them a new or different way, then they will fall into trouble. Let us see can we talk to one child today to stir them in the right direction. Enjoy your Saturday.

Time of Reflections

____

____

____

____

____

October 12

Its Sunday, Sing, Shouting, Praising God Sunday Morning! What are you expecting today? I will expect the blessings of God to be upon me this day. God is yet in the blessing business. I know that there is a miracle that is on the way for me. I decree and declare it now that the joy that I have the world didn't give it to me and the world can't take it away!

Time of Reflections

____

____

____

____

____

October 13

Moving Forward, Manifesting Monday! Psalm 140:12-13. I know that the Lord will maintain the cause of the afflicted, and the right of the poor. Surely the righteous shall give thanks unto thy name: the upright shall dwell in thy presence.

Time of Reflections

____

____

____

____

____

October 14

Trusting Him, Turning it around Tuesday! Psalm 141:1-2. Lord, I cry unto thee: make haste unto me; give ear unto my voice, when I cry unto thee. Let my prayer be set forth before thee as incense; and the lifting up of my hands as the evening sacrifice. Happy Birthday Mom: Jennie Pearl McNeill rest in peace this marks your 13th year of resting in Glory! We miss you and we will forever love you! Your Precious Children & Grands!

Time of Reflections

____

____

____

____

____

October 15

Waiting on the Lord, Willing to go all the way with the Lord Wednesday! Psalm 141:8-9. But mine eyes are unto thee, O god the Lord: in thee is my trust; leave not my soul destitute. Keep me from the snares which they have laid for me, and the gins of the workers of iniquity.

Time of Reflections

____

____

____

____

____

October 16

Triumphant, Take me through dear Lord take me through Thursday! Psalm 142:1-2. I cried unto the Lord with my voice; with my voice unto the Lord did I make my supplication. I poured out my complaint before him; I showed before him my trouble.

Time of Reflections

October 17

Faithful to Believe Friday! Psalm 142:5-6. I cried unto thee, O Lord: I said, Thou art my refuge and my portion in the land of the living. Attend unto my cry; for I am brought very low: deliver me from my persecutors; for thy are stronger than I.

Time of Reflections

October 18

Standing Still, Shaping Up Super Saturday! Psalm 143:1. Hear my prayer, O Lord, give ear to my supplications: in thy faithfulness answer me, and in thy righteousness.

Time of Reflections

____

____

____

____

____

October 19

Spirit Fall on Me, Standing on a sure Foundation Sunday! Psalm 143:7-8. Hear me speedily, O Lord: my spirit faileth: hide not thy face from me, lest I be like unto them that go down into the pit. Cause me to hear thy loving kindness in the morning; for in thee do I trust: cause me to know the way wherein I should walk; for I lift up my soul unto thee.

Time of Reflections

____

____

____

____

____

October 20

Mighty God is he, Moving Forward, Making me Happy and Making Me Whole Manifesting Monday! Psalm 143:10. Teach me to do thy will; for thou art my God: thy spirit is good; lead me into the land of uprightness.

Time of Reflections

October 21

Take Me Back, Trusting in him Tuesday! Psalm 144:1-2. Blessed be the Lord my strength, which teacheth my hands to war, and my fingers to fight: My goodness, and my fortress; my high tower, and my deliverer; my shield, and he in whom I trust; who subdueth my people under me.

Time of Reflections

October 22

Work it Out, Well With My Soul Worshipping Wednesday! Psalm 145:1-2. I will extol thee, my God, O king; and I will bless thy name for ever and ever. Every day will I bless thee; and I will praise thy name for ever and ever.

Time of Reflections

____

____

____

____

____

October 23

Through thick and thin, Trampling over the enemy Thursday! Psalm 145:7-8. They shall abundantly utter the memory of thy great goodness, and shall sing of thy righteous. The Lord is gracious, and full of compassion; slow to anger, and of great mercy.

Time of Reflections

____

____

____

____

____

October 24

Fret Not, Forgiven, Faithful to believe Friday! Psalm 145:9-10. The Lord is good to all: and his tender mercies are over all his works. All thy works shall praise thee, O Lord; and thy saints shall bless thee.

Time of Reflections

____

____

____

____

____

October 25

Shaking the Devil Off, Somebody had me on their Mind Super Saturday! Psalm 145:15-16. The eyes of all wait upon thee; and thou givest them their meat in due season. Thou openest thine hand, and satisfies the desire of every living thing.

Time of Reflections

____

____

____

____

____

October 26

Still Holding On, Stepping On, Save By Grace Sunday! Psalm 145:17-18. The Lord is righteous in all his ways, and holy in all his works. The Lord is night unto all them that call upon him, to all that call upon him in truth.

Time of Reflections

____

____

____

____

____

October 27

Making Me Happy and Making Me Whole Moving Forward, Making Away Monday! Psalm 145:21. My mouth shall speak the praise of the Lord; and let all flesh bless his holy name forever and ever.

Time of Reflections

____

____

____

____

____

October 28

Take me Back, Trusting in him, Telling the Devil I don't belong to him Tuesday! Psalm 146:1-2. Praise ye the Lord. Praise the Lord, O my soul. While I live will I praise the Lord: I will sing praises unto my God while I have any being.

Time of Reflections

October 29

Work it Out, Well with my Soul, Worshipping, Winning Wednesday! Psalm 147:1. Praise ye the Lord: for it is good to sing praises unto our God; for it is pleasant; and praise is comely.

Time of Reflections

October 30

Taking it to Jesus, Triumphant, Taking it Back Thursday! Psalm 147:3-5. He healeth the broken in heart, and bindeth up their wounds. He telleth the number of the stars; he calleth them all by their names. Great is our Lord, and of great power: his understanding is infinite.

Time of Reflections

____

____

____

____

____

October 31

Two Final things (1) Finally Friday & (2) Finally this month is ending! We give God praise and glory for what he has done and yet doing in the lives of his people. We must work out our own soul salvation with fear and trembling. We must be determined to hold out and hold on cause at the end we will win. Its like this either you are in a battle, getting ready to go into a battle, you coming out of a battle but I encourage each of you today, don't wait until the battle is over but shout now because God has given us that we needed to sustain us this day!

Time of Reflections

____

____

____

____

____

Month Eleven

November

November 1

Somebody Prayed for Me Super Saturday! Psalm 148:1-2. Praise ye the Lord, Praise ye the Lord from the heavens: praise him in the heights. Praise ye him, all his angels: praise ye him, all his hosts.

Time of Reflections

____

____

____

____

____

November 2

Still Holding On, Stepping Forward Sunday! Psalm 148:3-5. Praise ye him, sun and moon: praise him, all ye stars of light. Praise him, ye heavens of heavens, and ye waters that be above the heavens. Let them praise the name of the Lord: for he commanded, and they were created.

Time of Reflections

____

____

____

____

____

November 3

Moving Forward Manifesting, Miracle happening Monday! Psalm 148:13. Let them praise the name of the Lord: for his name alone is excellent; his glory is above the earth and heaven.

Time of Reflections

____

____

____

____

____

November 4

Trusting in Him, Turning it Around Tuesday! Psalm 149:1,4. Praise ye the Lord. Sing unto the Lord a new song, and his praise in the congregation of saints. For the Lord taketh pleasure in his people: he will beautify the meek with salvation. Man look out the outer appearance but God looks and knows the heart! How does your heart look today?

Time of Reflections

____

____

____

____

____

November 5

Working for Jesus, Willing to do his will, Worshipping, Winning Wednesday! Psalm 150. Praise ye the Lord. Praise God in his sanctuary: praise him in the firmament of his power. Praise him for his mighty acts; praise him according to his excellent greatness. Praise him with the sound of the trumpet: praise him with the psaltery and harp. Praise him with the timbrel and dance: praise him with stringed instruments and organs. Praise him upon the loud cymbals: praise him upon the high sounding cymbals. Let every thing that hath breath praise the Lord. Praise ye the Lord.

Time of Reflections

____

____

____

____

____

November 6

Triumphant taking it to Jesus Thursday! Proverbs 1:5,6. A wise man will hear, and will increase learning; and a man of understanding shall attain unto wise counsels: To understand a proverb, and the interpretation; the words of the wise, and their dark sayings.

Time of Reflections

____

____

____

____

____

November 7

Faithful to believe, Following after him, Fantastic Friday! Proverbs 1:7-8. The fear of the Lord is the beginning of knowledge: but fools despise wisdom and instruction. My son, hear the instruction of thy father, and forsake not the law of thy mother. Listen now and it will save you a whole lot of pain and suffering in the end. Hear and your soul shall live.

Time of Reflections

____

____

____

____

____

November 8

Shaping Up, Standing Still, Super Saturday! Proverbs 3:9-10. Honour the Lord with thy substance, and with the first-fruits of all thine increase: So shall thy barns be filled with plenty, and thy presses shall burst out with new wine. If you want to reap the harvest, then you must give God what is due to him cheerfully. Then in the end you will have plenty.

Time of Reflections

____

____

____

____

____

November 9

Spirit Fall on Me, Standing on a Sure Foundation, Shouting, Singing, Serving the Lord Sunday! Isaiah 12:1. Behold, god is my salvation; I will trust, and not be afraid: for the Lord JEHOVAH is my strength and my song; he also is become my salvation.

Time of Reflections

____

____

____

____

____

November 10

Making Me Happy & Making Me Whole Moving Forward Monday! Isaiah 53:1,4-5. Who hath believed our report? And to whom is the arm of the Lord revealed. Surely he hath borne our grief, and carried our sorrows: yet we did esteem him stricken, smitten of God, and afflicted. But he was wounded for our transgressions, he was bruised for our iniquities: the chastisement of our peace was upon him; and with his stripes we are healed. I shall believe the report of the Lord. I am healed already because the Word says so and I know that by Jesus' stripes I am healed already! What about you?

Time of Reflections

____

____

____

____

____

November 11

Take Time, Thanking God & all Veterans who served this wonderful country and nation. God bless each of you dearly and the families of those who lost love ones while fighting and standing up for our country. Isaiah 55:11. So shall my word be that goeth forth out of my mouth: it shall not return unto me void, but it shall accomplish that which I please, and it shall prosper in the thing whereto I sent it. Enjoy this take Me back, Trusting in Him Tuesday! I will trust in the Lord until I die.

Time of Reflections

____

____

____

____

____

November 12

Work it Out, Well Please, Worshipping and Winning Wednesday! Isaiah 61:1-2. The Spirit of the Lord God is upon me; because the Lord hath anointed me to preach good tidings unto the meek; he hath sent me to bind up the brokenhearted, to proclaim liberty to the captives, and the opening of the prison to them that are bound; to proclaim the acceptable year of the Lord, and the day of vengeance of our God; to comfort all that mourn.

Time of Reflections

____

____

____

____

____

November 13

Through thick and thin, Trampling over the enemy, Triumphant Thursday! Isaiah 65:17-18. For, behold, I create new heavens and a new earth: and the former shall not be remembered, nor come into mind. But be ye glad and rejoice for ever in that which I create: for, behold, I create Jerusalem a rejoicing, and her people a joy.

Time of Reflections

____

____

____

____

____

November 14

Fret Not, Forgiven, Faithful to Believe Friday! Malachi 3:10. Bring ye all the tithes into the storehouse, that there may be meat in mine house, and prove me now herewith, saith the Lord of host, if I will not open you the windows of heaven, and pour you out a blessing, that there shall not be room enough to receive it.

Time of Reflections

____

____

____

____

____

November 15

Shaking the Devil Off, Somebody had me on their Mind, Super Saturday! Habakkuk 2:2-3. And the Lord answered me, and said, Write the vision, and make it plain upon tables, that he may run that readeth it. For the vision is yet for an appointed time, but at the end it shall speak, and not lie: though it tarry, wait for it; because it will surely come, it will not tarry. I know for a fact "It Will Surely Come!" Let us continue to wait on the Lord and don't be weary because in due season we are going to reap if we faint not.

Time of Reflections

____

____

____

____

____

November 16

Still Holding On, Stepping Forward for the Master's Purpose Sunday! St. Matthew 4:17,19. From that time Jesus began to preach, and to say, Repent: for the kingdom of heaven is at hand. And he said unto them, Follow me, and I will make you fishers of men. Today is the day of salvation. Do not let the opportunity pass you by. While the blood is yet running warm in our veins, we have a chance to say yes Lord; yes to his will and to his way!

Time of Reflections

____

____

____

____

____

November 17

Moving Forward, Manifesting, Miracle Happening Monday! St. Matthew 5:18-19. For verily I say unto you, till heaven and earth pass, one jot or one tittle shall in no wise pass from the law, till all be fulfilled. Whosoever therefore shall break one of these least commandments, and shall teach men so, he shall be called the least in the kingdom of heaven: but whosoever shall do and teach them, the same shall be called great in the kingdom of heaven.

Time of Reflections

November 18

Trusting in Him, Turning it Around, Taking it Back Tuesday! St. Matthew 5:29-30. And if thy right eye offend thee, pluck it out, and cast it from thee: for it is profitable for thee that one of thy members should perish, and not that thy whole body should be cast into hell. And if thy right hand offend thee, cut it off, and cast it from thee: for it is profitable for thee that one of thy members should perish, and not that thy whole body should be cast into hell.

Time of Reflections

November 19

Worshipping, Working, Waiting on the Lord Wonderful Wednesday! St. Matthew 5:44-45. But I say unto you, Love your enemies, bless them that curse you, do good to them that hate you, and pray for them which despitefully use you, and persecute you; That ye may be the children of your Father which is in heaven: for he maketh his sun to rise on the evil and on the good, and sendeth rain on the just and on the unjust.

Time of Reflections

____

____

____

____

____

November 20

Triumphant, Taking it to Jesus Thursday! St. Matthew 6:19-21. Lay not up for yourselves treasures upon earth, where moth and rust doth corrupt, and where thieves break through and steal: but lay up for yourselves treasures in heaven, where neither moth nor rust doth corrupt, and where thieves do not break through nor steal: For where your treasure is, there will your heart be also.

Time of Reflections

____

____

____

____

____

November 21

Faithful to believe, Following Him, Fretting Not Fantastic Friday! St. Matthew 7:7-8. Ask, and it shall be given you; seek, and ye shall find; knock, and it shall be opened unto you: For everyone that asketh, receiveth; and he that seeketh, findeth; and to him that knocketh, it shall be opened. We know the plan so what are we going to do about it! Whatever you want we have to Ask, Seek, and Knock! The Lord will open and give it to us that what we ask for. He is doing a new thing and whatever we ask for, whatever we pray for it shall not be denied saith the Lord!

Time of Reflections

____

____

____

____

____

November 22

Shaping Up, Standing Still, Satan will not will, Super Saturday! St. Matthew 9:37,39. Then saith he unto his disciples, The harvest truly is plenteous, but the labourers are few; Pray ye therefore the Lord of the harvest, that he will send forth labourers into the harvest. There is plenty work to be done so when are you going to put your hands into it and work unto the Lord. Your hands are the only hands he has to get his work done. Only what we do for Christ is going to last!

Time of Reflections

____

____

____

____

____

November 23

Still Holding on, Stepping On, Serving God Sunday! St. Matthew 10:41-42. He that receiveth a prophet in the name of a prophet shall receive a prophet's reward; and he that receiveth a righteous man in the name of a righteous man shall receive a righteous man's reward. And whosoever shall give to drink unto one of these little ones a cup of cold water only in the name of a disciple, verily I say unto you, he shall in no wise lose his reward.

Time of Reflections

____

____

____

____

____

November 24

Making Me Happy and Making Me Whole, Moving Forward Monday! St. Matthew 11:28-30. Come unto me, all ye that labour and are heavy laden, and I will give you rest. Take my yoke upon you and learn of me; for I am meek and lowly in heart: and ye shall find rest unto your souls. For my yoke is easy, and my burden is light. What better way to be happy than going to Jesus and casting all our cares upon him! Move Forward and don't look back. God has a blessing with your name on it this day!

Time of Reflections

____

____

____

____

____

November 25

Take Me back, Trusting in Him, Thanking God for another Day Tuesday! St. Matthew 16:24-25. Then said Jesus unto his disciples, If any man will come after me, let him deny himself, and take up his cross, and follow me. For whosoever will save his life shall lose it: and whosoever will lose his life for my sake shall find it.

Time of Reflections

____

____

____

____

____

November 26

Worshipping, Winning, Want Turn Back nor Around Wednesday! St. Matthew 18:3-4. And said, Verily I say unto you, Except ye be converted, and become as little children, ye shall not enter into the kingdom of heaven. Whosoever therefore shall humble himself as this little child, the same is greatest in the kingdom of heaven. In order to make it in to the Kingdom of God; you must enter and come in the right way! Yes, Humble as a dear little Child!

Time of Reflections

____

____

____

____

____

November 27

Happy Thanksgiving to each of you on this Through Thick in Thin, I made it Trampling over the Enemy, Thanking God Thursday! St. Matthew 18:18-20. And Jesus came and spake unto them, saying, All power is given unto me in heaven and in earth. Go ye therefore, and teach all nations, baptizing them in the name of the father, and of the Son, and of the Holy Ghost: Teaching them to observe all things whatsoever I have commanded you: and lo, I am with you always, even unto the end of the world. Amen.

Time of Reflections

November 28

Fantasy Free Shopping, taking care of me, Faithful to Believe Friday! St. Mark 1:7-8. And preached, saying, There cometh one mightier than I after me, the latchet of whose shoes I am not worthy to stoop down and unloose. I indeed have baptized you with water: but he shall baptize you with the Holy Ghost. When we think we are not worthy, God says we are worthy! So whatever He tells us to do and calls us to do, then we need to do it!

Time of Reflections

November 29

Shaking the Devil Off, Somebody Prayed for Me Saturday! St. Mark 8:35-37. For whosoever will save his life shall lose it; but whosoever shall lose his life for my sake and the gospel's, the same shall save it. For what shall it profit a man, if he shall gain the whole world, and lose his own soul? Or what shall a man give in exchange for his soul?

Time of Reflections

____

____

____

____

____

November 30

Still Serving The Lord, Super, Shouting, Singing, Still Holding On Sunday! St. Mark 9:23,28-29. Jesus said unto him, If thou canst believe, all things are possible to him that believeth. And when he was come into the house, his disciples asked him privately, Why could not we cast him out? And he said unto them, This kind can come forth by nothing, but by prayer and fasting. We must continue to pray and fast to see the manifestation of the Lord in our lives. We will not die from fasting or making that sacrifice to God. Ask yourself how bad do you want it?

Time of Reflections

____

____

____

____

____

Month Twelve

DECEMBER

December 1

Making Me Happy and Making Me Whole Miracle Happening, Moving Forward Monday! St. Luke 8:46-48. And Jesus said, Somebody hath touched me: for I perceived that virture is gone out of me. And when the woman saw that she was not hid, she came trembling, and falling down before him, she declared unto him before all the people for what cause she had touched him, and how she was healed immediately. And he said unto her, Daughter, be of good comfort: thy faith hath made thee whole; go in peace. Let us reach out this Monday and touch him so we too can be made whole.

Time of Reflections

____

____

____

____

____

December 2

Take Me Back, Trusting in Him, Terrific Tuesday! St. Luke 16:13. No servant can serve two masters: for either he will hate the one, and love the other; or else he will hold to the one, and despise the other. Ye cannot serve God and mammon. Which one have you made up in your mind that you are going to serve? I will serve God anyhow until I die. He came that we may have life and have it more abundantly. In him we live and have our being!

Time of Reflections

____

____

____

____

____

December 3

Work it Out, Well Please, Worshipping Winning Wednesday! St. Luke 18:22. Now when Jesus heard these things, he said unto him, Yet lackest thou one thing: sell all that thou hast, and distribute unto the poor, and thou shalt have treasure in heaven: and come, follow me. Give it up for the cause of Christ. He will bless you beyond measures. I rather have Jesus than silver and gold.

Time of Reflections

____

____

____

____

____

December 4

Through thick and thin, Trampling over the Enemy Triumphant Thursday! St. Luke 22:31-32. And the Lord said, Simon, Simon, behold, Satan hath desired to have you, that he may sift you as wheat: But I have prayed for thee, that thy faith fail not: and when thou art converted, strengthen thy brethren.

Time of Reflections

____

____

____

____

____

December 5

Fret Not, Forgiven, Faithful to Believe Friday! St. Luke 23:39,42-43. And one of the malefactors which were hanged railed on him, saying, If thou be Christ, save thyself and us. And he said unto Jesus, Lord, remember me when thou comest into thy kingdom. And Jesus said unto him, Verily I say unto thee, Today, shalt thou be with me in praradise. The Lord will remember us, the point is how often will remember him? Don't leave no where without him he is more important than a discover card. It is important to me to be saved, it is important to me that my soul is set free, it's important to me to be saved.

Time of Reflections

____

____

____

____

____

December 6

Shaking the Devil Off, Somebody Prayed for Me, Super Saturday! St. John 1:1-2. In the beginning was the Word, and the Word was with God, and the Word was God. The same was in the beginning with god.

Time of Reflections

____

____

____

____

____

December 7

Sing, I thank God I am Saved, Sanctified, Holy Ghost Filled and Fired Baptized I got Jesus on my side and I am running for my life. Yes, it is another Super, Singing, Shouting, Serving God, Still Holding On Sunday! St. John 3:16. For God so loved the word, that he gave his only begotten Son, that whosoever believeth in him should not perish, but have everlasting life.

Time of Reflections

December 8

Moving Forward, Manifesting, Miracle Moving Monday! St. John 14:1-3. Let not your heart be troubled: ye believe in God, believe also in me. In my Father's house are many mansions: if it were not so, I would have told you. I go to prepare a place for you. And if I go and prepare a place for you, I will come again, and receive you unto myself; that where I am, there ye may be also.

Time of Reflections

December 9

Trusting In Him, Turning it Around Tuesday! Romans 8:28-29. And we know that all things work together for good to them that love God, to them who are called according to his purpose. For whom he did foreknow, he also did predestinate to be conformed to the image of his Son, that he might be the firstborn among many brethren.

Time of Reflections

____

____

____

____

____

December 10

Working For Jesus, Willing to do His Will, Working out my own soul Salvation Wonderful Wednesday! Romans 8:36-37. As it is written, For thy sake we are killed all the day long; we are accounted as sheep for the slaughter. Nay, in all these things we are more than conquerors through him that loved us. We are not just conquerors, but we are more than Conquerors! So be encouraged and continue to look up no matter what come or go.

Time of Reflections

____

____

____

____

____

December 11

Triumphant, Take Me to the King Thursday! Romans 12:1-2. I beseech you therefore, brethren, by the mercies of God, that ye present your bodies a living sacrifice, holy, acceptable unto God, which is your reasonable service. And be not conformed to this world: but be ye transformed by the renewing of your mind, that ye may prove what is that good, and acceptable, and perfect, will of God. We must be transformed by the renewing of our mind. That change will come once we let this mind be in us that is also in Christ Jesus our Lord! Hold On, Your Change is Coming, Hold On, Don't Worry About A Thing!

Time of Reflections

____

____

____

____

____

December 12

Faithful to Believe, Following Him, Fellowshipping Friday! I Corinthians 11:1-2. Be ye followers of me, even as I also am of Christ. Now I praise you, brethren, that ye remember me in all things, and keep the ordinances, as I delivered them to you. Its good to follow after certain thing, but the best thing and person you can follow after is the Spirit of God. It will lead you into all truth!

Time of Reflections

____

____

____

____

____

December 13

Shaping Up, Standing Still, Saying Yes to the Master's Holy Will Saturday! I Corinthians 13:1-2,4-7. Though I speak with the tongues of men and of angels, and have not charity, I am become as sounding brass, or a tinkling cymbal. And though I have the gift of prophecy, and understand all mysteries, and all knowledge; and though I have all faith, so that I could remove mountains, and have not charity, I am nothing. Charity suffereth long, and is kind; charity envieth not; charity vaunteth not itself, is not puffed up, Doth not behave itself unseemly, seeketh not her own, is not easily provoked, thinketh no evil; rejoiceth not in iniquity, but rejoiceth in the truth; Beareth all things, believeth all things, hopeth all things, endureth all things. Charity (LOVE) Has a Lot to do With It!

Time of Reflections

____

____

____

____

____

December 14

Spirit Fall On Me, Serving God, Standing on a Sure Foundation Sunday! I Corinthians 15:51-52,58. Behold, I show you a mystery; we shall not all sleep, but we shall all be changed, in a moment, in the twinkling of an eye, at the last trump: for the trumpet shall sound, and the dead shall be rasied incorruptible, and we shall be changed. Therefore, my beloved brethren, be ye steadfast, unmoveable, always abounding in the work of the Lord, forasmuch as ye know that your labor is not in vain in the Lord. We must be unmovable because everything is going down but the WORD of God. Be planted like the tree planted by the river of waters. NO, WE SHALL NOT BE MOVED!

Time of Reflections

____

____

____

____

____

December 15

Move Satan Move, More of Jesus and Less of Me, Moving Forward Monday! II Corinthians 5:1,6-7. For we know that if our earthly house of this tabernacle were dissolved, we have a building of God, an house not made with hands eternal in the heavens. Therefore we are always confident, knowing that, whilst we are at home in the body, we are absent from the Lord: For we walk by faith, not by sight.

Time of Reflections

____

____

____

____

____

December 16

Taking One Step at the Time, Tapping Into My Season, Thanking him, and Trusting Him Tuesday! Galatians 3:1-2. O Foolish Galatians, who hath bewitched you, that ye should not obey the truth, before whose eyes Jesus Christ hath been evidently set forth, crucified among you? This only would I learn of you, Received ye the Spirit by the works of the law, or by the hearing of faith.

Time of Reflections

____

____

____

____

____

December 17

Walk With Me Lord, Working for Jesus, Work It Out For Me Worshipping Wednesday! Galatians 5:1,5,7. Stand Fast therefore in the liberty wherewith Christ hath made us free, and be not entangled again with the yoke of bondage. For we through the Spirit wait for the hope of righteousness by faith. Ye did run well; who did hinder you that ye should not obey the truth?

Time of Reflections

____

____

____

____

____

December 18

Take Me to the King, Telling Satan No Deal, Triumphant Thursday! Galatians 6:1-2. Brethren, If a man be overtaken in a fault, ye which are spiritual, restore such an one in the spirit of meekness; considering thyself, lest thou also be tempted. Bear ye one another's burdens, and so fulfill the law of Christ.

Time of Reflections

____

____

____

____

____

December 19

Filled Up, Over Flowing, Free From Sin, Faithful to Believe Friday! Ephesians 6:10-12. Finally, my brethren, be strong in the Lord, and in the power of his might. Put on the whole armour of God, that ye may be able to stand against the wiles of the devil. For we wrestle not against flesh and blood, but against principalities, against powers, against the rulers of the darkness of this world, against spiritual wickedness in high places.

Time of Reflections

____

____

____

____

____

December 20

Satan thought he had me, Shake, Shake, Shake, Shake the Devil off, Shaping Up, Standing Still Super Saturday! Philippians 3:13-14. Brethren, I count not myself to have apprehended: but this one thing I do, forgetting those things which are behind, and reaching forth unto those things which are before, I press toward the mark for the prize of the high calling of God in Christ Jesus.

Time of Reflections

____

____

____

____

____

December 21

One Moment in God's Kingdom will pay for it all! Yes, another Serving God, Saying Yes to His Will, Shouting, Singing, So Determined Sunday! Philippians 4:12-13. I know how to be abased, and I know how to abound: everywhere and in all things I am instructed both to be full and to be hungry, both to abound and to suffer need. I can do all things through Christ which strengthened me.

Time of Reflections

____

____

____

____

____

December 22

Make Every Step Count, Moving Forward, Miracle Moving, Marching On Monday! Colossians 3:12-13,17. Put on therefore, as the elect of God, holy and beloved, bowels of mercies, kindness, humbleness of mind, meekness, longsuffering; forbearing one another, and forgiving one another, if any man have a quarrel against any; even as Christ forgave you, so also do ye. And whatsoever ye do in word or deed, do all in the name of the Lord Jesus, giving thanks to God and the Father by him.

Time of Reflections

____

____

____

____

____

December 23

Take it to Jesus, Telling of His Goodness, Trying to Make it, Tried by The Fire Tuesday! II Timothy 4:6-8. For I am now ready to be offered, and the time of my departure is at hand. I have fought a good fight, I have finished my course, I have kept the faith. Henceforth there is laid up for me a crown of righteousness, which the Lord, the righteous judge, shall give me at that day: and not to me only, but unto all them also that love his appearing.

Time of Reflections

____

____

____

____

____

December 24

Happy Christmas Eve to all of you! What better way to celebrate this Holiday but through the eyes of Faith! We all want something for Christmas and we may not see anything even now but we are keeping the faith that something will be here for us. Hebrews 11:1-2. Now faith is the substance of things hoped for, the evidence of things not seen. For by it the elders obtained a good report. Faith, Faith just a little more faith we don't need a whole lot we just need to use what we got, Faith, Faith just a little more faith.

Time of Reflections

____

____

____

____

____

December 25

Merry Christmas to each of You! Merry Christmas and Happy Birthday to JESUS! The Savior of the World. St. Luke 2:9-11,14. And, lo, the angel of the Lord came upon them, and the glory of the Lord shone round about them: and they were sore afraid. And the angel said unto them, Fear not: for, behold, I bring you good tidings of great joy, which shall be to all people. For unto you is born this day in the city of David a Savior, which is Christ the Lord. Glory to God in the highest, and on earth peace, good will toward all men. I hope this be a bless Christmas for each of you God bless you abundantly this day and everyday on this Triumphant Thursday!

Time of Reflections

____

____

____

____

____

December 26

Faithful to Believe Friday! Hebrews 12:1-2. Wherefore seeing we also are compassed about with so great a cloud of witnesses, let us lay aside every weight, and the sin which doth so easily beset us, and let us run with patience the race that is set before us, Looking unto Jesus the author and finisher of our faith; who for the joy that was set before him endured the cross, despising the shame, and is set down at the right hand of the throne of God. The race is not given to the swift nor to the strong but he that endure until the end. So I encourage each of us to stay in the race don't stop nor give up! We are going to make it.

Time of Reflections

____

____

____

____

____

December 27

Say, I come too far by Faith, Leaning on the Lord! Yes it is Shaping Up, Standing Still, Seeing the Salvation of the Lord Saturday! James 1:2-5. My brethren, count it all joy when ye fall into divers temptations; knowing this, that the trying of your faith worketh patience. But let patience have her perfect work, that ye may be perfect and entire, wanting nothing. If any of you lack wisdom, let him ask of god, that giveth to all men liberally, and upbraideth not; and it shall be given him.

Time of Reflections

____

____

____

____

____

December 28

Spirit fall on Me, Searching for My Jesus, Standing on a Sure Foundation, Praising and Serving My Savior all the daylong Sunday! I Peter 4:12-13. Beloved, think it not strange concerning the fiery trial which is to try you, as though some strange thing happened unto you: But rejoice, inasmuch as ye are partakers of Christ's sufferings; that, when his glory shall be revealed, ye may be glad also with exceeding joy. Enjoy this last Sunday in this year of 2014. I hope and trust it was a bless and prosperous year for each of you. God has smile on us and he has blessed us! Guess what? He is not through blessing you yet either!

Time of Reflections

____

____

____

____

____

December 29

Miracle Moving, Mighty God We Serve, Making Every Step Count, Moving Forward Monday! Revelation 7:13-14. And one of the elders answered, saying unto me, What are these which are arrayed in white robes? And whence came they? And I said unto him, Sir, thou knowest. And he said to me, These are they which came out of great tribulation, and have washed their robes, and made them white in the blood of the Lamb. Can you say, that in the year of 2014 that God has brought us out of Great Tribulation and Brought us from a mighty long ways! What kind of God would do this for me, incredible God deserves incredible praise as we close out this year!

Time of Reflections

____

____

____

____

____

December 30

One more day and we will be closing this year out! What you didn't get done this year, ask God to help you to do more and better in 2015. Wow! Can you believe that we aer out of this year almost and going into another one. Revelation 22:12-13. And, behold I come quickly; and my reward is with me, to give every man according as his work shall be. I am Alpha and Omega, the beginning and the end, the first and the last.

Time of Reflections

____

____

____

____

____

December 31

Its over now, Its over now, I feel like we have made it because 2014 is almost out. Even in the last minute before the year is out someone will be called into judgment. Just make sure that we are ready to meet our GOD! What a way to close out this year on a Worshipping, Willing to do his Will, Waiting On Jesus, Wonderful Wednesday! Revelations 22:19-21. And if any man shall take away from the words of the book of this prophecy, God shall take away his part out of the book of life, and out of the holy city, and from the things which are written in this book. He which testifieth these things, saith, Surely I come quickly. Amen. Even so, come, Lord Jesus. The grace of our Lord Jesus Christ be with you all Amen.

Time of Reflections

Conclusion

Thank you for allowing me to spend 365 days with you through God Goodness! I hope and trust that this "Daily Reflections" has truly been a blessing to you. As you could reflect daily of the things that you encountered in your life. But through it all, God brought you and prayerfully you are wiser, stronger, encouraged and more determined to MOVE FORWARD. God has a plan for you and you are Destined to reach it! Be encouraged and know that God is Concerned and He is Working Things Out For You!

Love,
Demonn McNeill